GOD'S MASTERWORK

A Concerto in Sixty-Six Movements

Volume Five

2 Thessalonians through Revelation

From the Bible-teaching ministry of

CHARLES R. SWINDOLL

INSIGHT FOR LIVING

Chuck graduated in 1963 from Dallas Theological Seminary, where he now serves as the school's fourth president, helping to prepare a new generation of men and women for the ministry. Chuck has served in pastorates in three states: Massachusetts, Texas, and California, including almost twenty-three years at the First Evangelical Free Church in Fullerton, California. His sermon messages have been aired over radio since 1979 as the *Insight for Living* broadcast. A best-selling author, Chuck has written numerous books and booklets on many subjects.

Based on the outlines and transcripts of Chuck's sermons, the study guide text is coauthored by Gary Matlack, a graduate of Texas Tech University and Dallas Theological Seminary, and by Bryce Klabunde, a graduate of Biola University and Dallas Theological Seminary. They also wrote the Living Insights sections.

Editor in Chief:
Cynthia Swindoll

Coauthors of Text:
Gary Matlack
Bryce Klabunde

**Senior Editor and
Assistant Writer:**
Wendy Peterson

Assistant Editor:
Glenda Schlahta

Copy Editors:
Deborah Gibbs   Tom Kimber
Marco Salazar   Karene Wells

Cover Designer:
Nina Paris

Text Designer:
Gary Lett

Publishing System Specialist:
Alex Pasieka

Director, Communications Division:
John Norton

Marketing Manager:
Alene Cooper

Project Coordinator:
Shannon Scharkey

Production Coordinator:
Don Bernstein

Printer:
Sinclair Printing Company

Unless otherwise identified, all Scripture references are from the New American Standard Bible, © The Lockman Foundation 1960, 1962, 1963, 1968, 1971, 1972, 1973, 1975, 1977, 1995. Used by permission. Scripture taken from the Holy Bible, New International Version © 1973, 1978, 1984 International Bible Society, used by permission of Zondervan Bible Publishers.

Guide coauthored by Gary Matlack and Bryce Klabunde:
Copyright © 1998 by Charles R. Swindoll, Inc.

Original outlines, charts, and transcripts:
Copyright © 1982, 1983 by Charles R. Swindoll, Inc.

Unless otherwise indicated, all charts are adapted from *The Living Insights Study Bible*, copyright © 1996 by the Zondervan Corporation.

An effort has been made to locate sources and obtain permission where necessary for the quotations used in this book. In the event of any unintentional omission, a modification will gladly be incorporated in future printings.

Series ISBN 0-8499-1474-4—*God's Masterwork: A Concerto in Sixty-Six Movements*
Study guide ISBN 0-8499-8742-3—*Volume Five: 2 Thessalonians–Revelation*
COVER IMAGE: International Stock
COVER BACKGROUND PHOTO: Superstock
Printed in the United States of America

CONTENTS

INTRODUCTION

I remember hearing about an extremist group that thought they had calculated the exact date of Christ's return.

They put on white robes, climbed up on their rooftops . . . and waited. Day after day, through the midday heat and cool of the night, they waited. And He did not come. Finally, they slid down off their roofs in embarrassment.

Jesus is coming back; that's for certain. But He never gave us the date—probably because He knew many of us would respond like the people described above. Yes, God wants us to live each day in anticipation of Christ's return. But we need to live vital, productive lives while we're here.

Once again we see how an understanding of the Bible—or a misunderstanding of it—affects our lives. In this, our final volume of *God's Masterwork*, we'll ponder Christ's second coming and a variety of other themes as they appear in these last fourteen books of the Bible.

So finish well, fellow Christian. And may the entire *God's Masterwork* series lead you to a deeper understanding of God's Word and a deeper love for your Savior.

Chuck Swindoll

PUTTING TRUTH INTO ACTION

K nowledge apart from application falls short of God's desire for His children. He wants us to apply what we learn so that we will change and grow. This study guide was prepared with these goals in mind. As you go through the following pages, we hope your desire to discover biblical truth will grow as your understanding of God's Word increases and that you will be encouraged to apply what you've learned.

To assist you in your study, we've included a section called **Living Insights** at the end of each lesson. These exercises will challenge you to study further and to think of specific ways to put your discoveries into action.

There are many ways to use this guide—in personal devotions, group studies, discussions with friends and family, and Sunday school classes. And, of course, it's an ideal study aid when you're listening to its corresponding *Insight for Living* radio series.

To benefit most from this study guide, we would encourage you to consider it a spiritual journal. That's why we've included space in the **Living Insights** for recording your thoughts and discoveries. We hope you'll return to those sections often for review and encouragement as you continue to grow in your walk with Christ.

Bryce Klabunde
Coauthor of Text
Author of Living Insights

Gary Matlack
Coauthor of Text
Author of Living Insights

GOD'S MASTERWORK

A Concerto in Sixty-Six Movements

Volume Five

2 Thessalonians through Revelation

2 THESSALONIANS: CHRIST'S COMING... MY RESPONSE

A Survey of 2 Thessalonians

Good theology is like a ship's ballast, it keeps us from listing too far to port or starboard and holds us on a steady course toward serving Christ. Bad theology, however, tends to pull us to extremes and can shipwreck us spiritually.

The Thessalonian believers had received some bad theology about Christ's return, and it had dealt their spiritual equilibrium a serious blow. They were already suffering intense persecution for their faith, and this misinformation only added to their stress. Paul wrote 2 Thessalonians to encourage them in their present situation and adjust their thinking about the end times.

Background of 2 Thessalonians

In 1 Thessalonians, Paul had told his readers about both the Rapture—the time when Christ would appear and gather His followers to Himself—and the Day of the Lord (1 Thess. 4:13–5:11).[1] He had encouraged them to stand firm in the Lord and live in quiet anticipation of Christ's return.

---

1. The Old Testament reveals the Day of the Lord as the time God will judge the nations and pour out His wrath on the earth (Joel 2:1–2, 31–32; Obad. 15–16; Zeph. 1:14–18). Many Bible scholars associate this judgment period with Daniel's "seventieth week," a seven-year span of turmoil in which an evil prince will rise to power, then be destroyed (Dan. 9:24–27). Jesus echoed Daniel's prophecy in His teaching, calling this time a "tribulation," which will culminate in His second coming (Matt. 24:4–31, see also Rev. 19:11–21).

2 THESSALONIANS

	Affirmation Amidst Affliction	Explanation of Prophecy	Clarification regarding Response
	"We ought always to give thanks to God for you." (1:3) "We . . . speak proudly of you . . . for your perseverance and faith." (1:4) "We pray for you always." (1:11)	"Let no one in any way deceive you." (2:3) Secret power of lawlessness Restraint removed Man of lawlessness "So then . . . stand firm." (2:15)	"We command you." (3:6) "If anyone does not obey . . ." (3:14) "May the Lord of peace Himself continually grant you peace." (3:16)
	CHAPTER 1	CHAPTER 2	CHAPTER 3
Question	Why are we suffering?	What will occur?	How do I respond?
Contrasts	Peace amidst pain	Lawlessness versus restraint	Work while waiting
Statement	The Lord knows!	The "day of the Lord" has not yet come!	"Do not grow weary of doing good." (3:13)
Emphasis	Commendation	Correction	Clarification
Main Theme	The hope of Christ's return encourages us in our suffering and motivates us to live responsibly for Him.		
Key Verses		1:11–12; 2:13–15	

2

Unfortunately, either through a vision, a sermon, or a fraudulent letter presented as Paul's, wild rumors were spreading that the Day of the Lord had already come. The Thessalonians' persecution only confirmed the fears of many that God was about to unleash His wrath on the earth and that their meager faith would not be able to stand the test. Others, however, anticipating the end, had quit their jobs and become idle busybodies, living on handouts and burdening others.

Overview of the Letter

So Paul penned a second letter to shore up their faith and set them straight. His letter has three sections, which correspond to its three chapters. First, Paul affirms the Thessalonian believers' faith in the midst of affliction. Next, he explains the prophecy they had been misinformed about. Finally, he clarifies the proper response to the truth about Christ's return.

Affirmation amidst Affliction (Chap. 1)

After bestowing grace and peace on the Thessalonians from both the Father and the Son (vv. 1–2), Paul thanks God for their maturing faith and love (v. 3).[2] He tells them how proud he is that they've persevered under persecution (v. 4). And then he reminds them that they are not suffering for a fading earthly prize but for something greater: the kingdom of God (v. 5).

Despite the injustices the Thessalonian believers face daily, Paul reassures them that God is still just. One day, Christ will come with His mighty angels and set right all the wrongs in the world. Retribution will come to the afflicters, and relief will come to the afflicted (vv. 6–7). Paul includes a frightening picture of hell for unbelievers, those who have persecuted His people: they will suffer eternally, forever separated from the presence of God—the presence of all that's good and all that's worthwhile (vv. 8–9). Unlike those separated from God's glory are the faithful, in whom Christ will be glorified forever (v. 10).

Among those faithful are the Thessalonians, and Paul next offers the first of four prayers on their behalf (vv. 11–12; see also

2. Notice that the Thessalonians had faith and love; it was their hope that was shaky.

2:16–17; 3:5, 16).[3] He asks God to help these believers live up to their calling so that Christ will be glorified in them. For it's Christ's glory that should be the goal of every desire, every work, every experience—even every time of suffering—we have. Because that's the only proper outworking of God's abounding grace in our lives.

Explanation of Prophecy (Chap. 2)

With their faith and love affirmed, Paul now turns to clarify their hope (2:1). They were reeling from the false message that "the day of the Lord has come" (2:2). To settle the Thessalonians' fears, Paul describes the Day of the Lord to prove that it hasn't already arrived.

The first sign of the Day of the Lord is *the apostasy* (v. 3a), which is a worldwide rebellion against God. In the last days, the nations will shake their fists at God in total defiance. Out of this evil climate will emerge one person who will lead the world in its wicked rebellion: the *man of lawlessness*, also known as the Antichrist (vv. 3b–5, 8–10a).[4] This false messiah will be "as much the incarnation of evil as Jesus was the incarnation of God."[5] In blasphemous contempt, he will exalt himself

> above every so-called god or object of worship, so that he takes his seat in the temple of God, displaying himself as being God. (v. 4)

Only one force keeps "the mystery of lawlessness" from overrunning the world with evil: *the restrainer.*

> And you know what restrains him now, so that in his time he will be revealed. For the mystery of lawlessness is already at work; only he who now restrains will do so until he is taken out of the way. (vv. 6–7)

Who is the "restrainer"? None other than the Holy Spirit, as commentator Thomas L. Constable explains.

3. There are more prayers per chapter in 2 Thessalonians than any of Paul's longer letters, which says a lot about his pastoral feelings for these people.

4. This individual goes by many names in Scripture: the little horn (Dan. 7:8, 24–26), the prince (9:26–27), the king (11:36–45), the antichrist (1 John 2:18), the beast (Rev. 13:1–10), the man of lawlessness, the son of destruction (2 Thess. 2:3).

5. William Barclay, *The Letters to the Philippians, Colossians, and Thessalonians*, rev. ed., The Daily Study Bible series (Philadelphia, Pa.: Westminster Press, 1975), p. 212.

The Holy Spirit of God is the only Person with sufficient (supernatural) power to do this retraining. . . . How does He do it? Through Christians, whom He indwells and through whom He works in society to hold back the swelling tide of lawless living. How will He be taken out of the way? When the church leaves the earth in the Rapture . . . His unique lawlessness-restraining ministry through God's people will be removed.[6]

Once that happens, nothing will stand in the way of the "son of destruction" coming to power.

The final feature of the Day of the Lord concerns the *judgment of unbelievers* (vv. 10–12). God will turn over to their sinful choices all who have loved what is false rather than what is true. In place of His Spirit's influence, He will send a "deluding influence." As a result, they will remain in the satanic lies they've already chosen and come under God's full judgment when Christ returns.

Thankfully, believers have a far brighter future—heaven. Paul writes,

But we should always give thanks to God for you, brethren beloved by the Lord, because God has chosen you from the beginning for salvation through sanctification by the Spirit and faith in the truth. It was for this He called you through our gospel, that you may gain the glory of our Lord Jesus Christ. (vv. 13–14)

These two statements about our salvation have been called "'a system of theology in miniature.'"[7] Commentator John Stott explores the marvelous truths of our redemption based on these verses.

In the eternity of the past God chose us to be saved. Then he called us in time, causing us to hear the

6. Thomas L. Constable, "2 Thessalonians," in *The Bible Knowledge Commentary*, New Testament edition, ed. John F. Walvoord and Roy B. Zuck (Wheaton, Ill.: Scripture Press Publications, Victor Books, 1983), p. 719.

7. James Denney, *The Epistles to the Thessalonians* (Expositor's Bible; Hodder and Stoughton, 1902), p. 342; as quoted by John Stott in *The Gospel and the End of Time: The Message of 1 and 2 Thessalonians* (Downers Grove, Ill.: InterVarsity Press, 1991), p. 175.

gospel, believe the truth and be sanctified by the Spirit, with a view to our sharing Christ's glory in the eternity of the future. In a single sentence the apostle's mind sweeps from "the beginning" to "the glory." There is no room in such a conviction for fears about Christian instability. Let the devil mount his fiercest attack on the feeblest saint, let the Antichrist be revealed and the rebellion break out, yet over against the instability of our circumstances and our characters, we set the eternal stability of the purpose of God.[8]

"So then," Paul says, "stand firm" (v. 15). Stand firm in the truth of your security in God and hold fast to true and reliable doctrine, Paul urges. We are to *live* these truths God has shown us.

To help us do that, Paul prays that God's eternal comfort and hope would settle in our hearts, strengthening us to do the good He has created us for (vv. 16–17).

Clarification of Our Response (Chap. 3)

Closing his thoughts in chapter 3, Paul leaves his readers with two final exhortations, each concluding with a prayer. First, Paul asks the Thessalonians to pray that the Gospel would meet with success and that he would be delivered from those who work for the Gospel's defeat (vv. 1–2). Emphasizing God's faithfulness, he reminds them that it is God who strengthens and protects them in their persecution (vv. 3–4). In the midst of such instability, Paul prays (v. 5) that their lives will be characterized by an inner awareness of "the love of God"—which provides security—and an outer expression of "the steadfastness of Christ"—which produces stability.

Moving from the external persecution, Paul addresses the discipline problem within the church. He exhorts those idly waiting for Christ's return to return to work and to personal responsibility (vv. 6–12). He also encourages the rest of the church to "not grow weary of doing good" and to admonish the disobedient (in love) to act in a more orderly manner (vv. 13–15).

He ends this section with the fourth prayer of his letter:

Now may the Lord of peace Himself continually

8. Stott, *The Gospel and the End of Time*, p. 177.

grant you peace in every circumstance. The Lord be
with you all! (v. 16)

For the Thessalonians, who were suffering at the cruel hand of
persecutors and the unsettling hand of end-times manipulators, the
peace of the Lord was a precious gift. But Christ offers more than
His peace; He offers His presence.

As if to emphasize this, Paul writes in his "own hand" one more
line: "The grace of our Lord Jesus Christ *be with you all*" (vv. 17–18,
emphasis added). Christ's ever-present grace—now that's something to stand firm in!

 Living Insights

Paul prayed that Jesus would grant the Thessalonians the same
gift He gave the disciples on the night before He went to the cross:

> "Peace I leave with you; My peace I give to you; not
> as the world gives do I give to you. Do not let your
> heart be troubled, nor let it be fearful." (John 14:27)

The peace the world gives is conditional. *If* we're healthy, *if* we
have money in the bank, *if* we're secure in our relationships, only
then can we say, "I'm at peace."

Jesus, however, gives a supernatural peace that is independent
of our circumstances. It's an "in-the-midst-of" peace. In the midst
of sickness. In the midst of financial stress. In the midst of relational
struggles.

"The heart that has this kind of peace is like a lighthouse in a
storm," writes author John White.

> Winds shriek, waves crash, lightning flickers around
> it. But inside, the children play while their parents
> go about their work. They may look out the window
> to marvel at the powers that rage around them, but
> they have peace—the peace of knowing that the
> strength which protects them is stronger than the
> strength of the storm.[9]

9. John White, *Greater than Riches: Daily Readings to Enrich Your Walk with God* (Downers
Grove, Ill.: InterVarsity Press, 1992), p. 131.

Are you in the midst of a storm? What winds and waves are threatening your peace?

_____

_____

_____

Based on the following verses, what reassurances do we have in the midst of our storms?

2 Thessalonians 1:6–7 _____

_____

2:13–14 _____

_____

3:3 _____

_____

3:16 _____

_____

Which of these truths speak the most directly to your situation?

_____

_____

It's one thing to know that the Lord is faithful and that He is with you always. It's quite another to put your trust completely in Him. Take a moment to examine your heart. Are there some fears hindering you from receiving the gift of peace Christ offers? Write them down; then take them to God in prayer, asking His help in opening those frightened, closed places to the healing of His grace.

_____

_____

_____

_____

Chapter 2

1 TIMOTHY: WISE COUNSEL FOR SHEPHERDS

A Survey of 1 Timothy

Survive.

That's what some people do in their spare time. Seriously. They spend their vacations pitting themselves against the unknowns of nature. Perhaps you've heard about, or even participated in, one of these "wilderness adventures." It's an amazing concept. Basically, you pay a fee to have yourself dropped in the middle of nowhere with nothing but a bowie knife and a bag of trail mix. Then it's *adiós, amigo*; you're on your own.

Overseeing the church sometimes seems like a wilderness adventure too. Pastors and other church leaders, dropped in the middle of never-ending needs with nothing but a clean suit and a seminary degree, often feel as inadequate as city slickers abandoned in the outback.

Fortunately, God has given us a guidebook on how to "do" church. Paul's first letter to Timothy provides inspired instructions for teaching, selecting leadership, and meeting peoples' needs. First Timothy is must reading for anyone who wants to minister God's way—and anyone who wants to not only survive ministry but succeed in it.

The Pastoral Epistles

First Timothy, 2 Timothy, and Titus make up the Pastoral Epistles. Unlike most of Paul's letters, which were addressed to entire churches, these three letters provided doctrinal, organizational, and personal instruction for individuals involved in the daily grind of ministry. Paul penned all three letters toward the end of his life. They are God's revelation for ministry, but they're enriched with Paul's lifetime of in-the-trenches service.

Paul and Timothy

The letter of 1 Timothy glows with the flame of a torch beginning to pass from the apostle Paul's hand to that of his friend and

9

1 TIMOTHY

	Personal Encouragement and Exhortation	The Ministry	The Minister
	Timothy's task	Men and women (2) (Prayer and submission)	**Seeing the importance of (4):** Faithful teaching — True godliness; Sound doctrine — Perseverance
	Paul's testimony Gospel's trustworthiness	Elders and deacons (3) (Qualifications for leadership)	**Paying attention to (5):** Various age groups — Elders; Widows — Wisdom
			Developing a new perspective toward (6): Masters and slaves — Internals and externals; Rich and poor — Eternal vs. temporal
	CHAPTER 1	CHAPTERS 2-3	CHAPTERS 4-6
Emphasis	The work of ministry		The one who ministers
Command	Be true!	Be wise!	Be strong and faithful!
Main Theme	Leadership of the church, the household of God		
Key Verse	"I'm writing these things to you, hoping to come to you before long; but in case I am delayed, I write so that you will know how one ought to conduct himself in the household of God, which is the church of the living God, the pillar and support of the truth." (3:14-15)		

protégé, Timothy, whom he had known for perhaps as many as twenty years. Commentator A. Duane Litfin tells how the lives of the two men became intertwined.

> Timothy was the son of a Greek father and Jewish mother (Acts 16:1). No mention is made of his father being a Christian, but his mother Eunice and grandmother Lois were both known for their sincere faith (2 Tim. 1:5). Timothy was no doubt living at Lystra when Paul visited that city on his first missionary journey (cf. Acts 14:6; 16:1). Whether or not Paul led Timothy to Christ cannot be known with certainty. At any rate Timothy already knew and believed the Old Testament Scriptures, thanks to his mother and grandmother (cf. 2 Tim. 3:15), and Paul took him on as a promising protégé. Paul thus became like a spiritual father to the young man, referring to him as "my true son in the faith" (1 Tim. 1:2) and "my dear son" (2 Tim. 1:2; cf. Phil. 2:22).[1]

Early on, Timothy displayed great promise as a minister of the Gospel. Recognizing his giftedness and potential, Paul "took him on as a companion and he became one of the apostle's most trustworthy fellow-laborers."[2] Timothy also served as Paul's representative and messenger to other churches when he couldn't be there personally. So trusted and capable was Timothy that Paul left him in Ephesus to lead that thriving church.

What, then, do you tell your understudy when you realize your time is almost up? What else but the things closest to your heart. For Paul, that meant the purity of the Gospel and the progress of Christ's church. So he wrote to Timothy, perhaps from Philippi, to deepen him in the message and ministry of the church, God's household (1 Tim. 3:15).

---

1. A. Duane Litfin, "1 Timothy," in *The Bible Knowledge Commentary*, New Testament edition, ed. John F. Walvoord and Roy B. Zuck (Wheaton, Ill.: Scripture Press Publications, Victor Books, 1983), pp. 729–30.

2. Litfin, "1 Timothy," p. 730.

Style and Structure of 1 Timothy

Though written to Paul's dear friend and ministry partner, 1 Timothy

> is rich in principles that are relevant to every Christian worker and Christian church. Because it was written to Timothy, this epistle assumes rather than develops doctrine. Its primary concern is with the practical outworking of Christian truth on an individual and corporate level. First Timothy, along with Titus, provides the most explicit directions for church leadership and organization in the Bible.[3]

This letter falls into three main sections. Chapter 1 focuses on Paul's *personal encouragement and exhortation* to Timothy. Chapters 2–3 emphasize the work of *the ministry*. And chapters 4–6 deal with the duties of *the minister*.

Personal Encouragement and Exhortation (Chap. 1)

> Paul, an apostle of Christ Jesus according to the commandment of God our Savior, and of Christ Jesus, who is our hope.
> To Timothy, my true child in the faith: Grace, mercy and peace from God the Father and Christ Jesus our Lord. (1 Tim. 1:1–2)

Paul's letter, as we can see, is no impersonal manual cranked out by the apostolic press. No, Paul's words flow out of a deep relationship with Timothy, his spiritual son. The two men had ministered together, rejoiced together, and suffered for the Gospel together. Now Paul had assigned Timothy to the Ephesian church, a thriving metropolitan congregation. No doubt overwhelmed at times by his responsibilities, Timothy needed some encouragement from his spiritual mentor.

Timothy's Task

Paul had urged Timothy in person, and now urges him by letter, to

---

3. Bruce Wilkinson and Kenneth Boa, *Talk Thru the Bible* (Nashville, Tenn.: Thomas Nelson Publishers, 1983), p. 429.

remain on at Ephesus so that you may instruct certain men not to teach strange doctrines, nor to pay attention to myths and endless genealogies, which give rise to mere speculation rather than furthering the administration of God which is by faith. (vv. 3b–4)

"Stay at it, Timothy. Maintain the purity of the Gospel. Answer false doctrine with truth." That's the heart of Paul's exhortation. Ephesus was the center of worship for the goddess Artemis (also called Diana), and this idolatry had to be exposed and refuted for the Ephesian church to remain healthy. Also constantly threatening to creep into the church were the Judaizers' counterfeit gospels, which exalted human works and wisdom and required keeping the Law. Paul clarifies the proper place of the Law and shows that the true Gospel results in love, not controversy (vv. 5–11).

The Gospel's Transforming Power

It is the message of Christ, after all, not humanly concocted religion, that changes lives to the glory of God. And Paul's life was a living trophy of Christ's transforming power (vv. 12–17). Confident that Christ saves people and equips them for ministry, Paul reminds Timothy to "fight the good fight" of faith in His strength, "keeping faith and a good conscience" even when others fall (vv. 18–20).

The Ministry (Chaps. 2–3)

Having exhorted Timothy to stay at his task, Paul now turns his attention to the myriad of responsibilities within Timothy's sphere of ministry.

The Priority of Prayer

First of all, then, I urge that entreaties and prayers, petitions and thanksgivings, be made on behalf of all men, for kings and all who are in authority, so that we may lead a tranquil and quiet life in all godliness and dignity. (2:1–2)

"First of all." It's no surprise that prayer occupies a priority position in Paul's thinking. Frequently in his letters, Paul acknowledges his total dependence on God, and he often mentions that he is praying for those who receive his letters.

Notice for whom Timothy and the church are to pray: for "all men" (2:1), which would include all people within and outside the family of God; and for "kings and all who are in authority" (v. 2). This is no cavalier suggestion for generic prayer. Here Paul is talking about prayer that drives the advancement of the Gospel—the message of the Mediator between God and man, Jesus Christ (vv. 3–7). Men particularly are to model and lead in the exercise of prayer (v. 8).

The Ministry of Women

And what about women? How are they to serve in the church? To begin with, says Paul, they should be noticed for their "good works" of godliness (v. 10), rather than their attire (v. 9). Paul isn't discouraging tasteful makeup, attractive jewelry, or nicely arranged fashions and accessories. His concern is that glitter and gaudiness not replace godliness. Character, not clothes, make the woman.

And what better place to display godly character than in the worship service, "quietly receiv[ing] instruction" (v. 11) instead of teaching or exercising authority over men (v. 12).

Contrary to some contemporary accusations, Paul's commands here are not sexist. He does not intend to gag women or prevent them from using their gifts and abilities for the good of the church and the glory of God. In terms of position in Christ and preciousness to Him, men have no advantage over women; all of us are equal in Christ (see Gal. 3:28). Rather, based on the order of Creation and the order of Adam and Eve's sin (1 Tim. 2:13–14), Paul is urging men to fulfill their God-appointed role of leading the church—and urging the women to let them lead. One of the problems at Ephesus may have been that the men weren't leading as they should, and the women were usurping that role.

The Offices of Elder and Deacon

Not every man, however, automatically qualifies to lead the church just by virtue of his gender. A leader's spiritual maturity and character must be of the highest quality.

Paul's list of qualifications covers every aspect of a man's life: personal, public, and home. A man who aspires to be an elder ("overseer," 3:1) must be "above reproach," that is, of sound reputation (v. 2). His life should be marked by attitudes and actions reflective of Christ. He should know the Scriptures well enough to teach them; his home should be characterized by harmony, order, and loving leadership; and he should be mature in the faith, known for his integrity in the church as well as outside it (vv. 4–7).

Deacons, likewise, should be selected according to their character, not randomly recruited (vv. 8–10, 12–13). And deaconesses are called to a high standard of personal discipline and spiritual maturity as well (v. 11).[4]

The Household of God

As though he's concerned that Timothy might be getting lost in all the details, Paul pauses to remind him why he's writing.

> I am writing these things to you, hoping to come to you before long; but in case I am delayed, I write so that you will know how one ought to conduct himself in the household of God, which is the church of the living God, the pillar and support of the truth. (vv. 14–15)

Proper conduct in the household of God. That's what 1 Timothy is all about. And that doesn't just mean keeping the kids from fidgeting in the pew. God's household is a family—the family of the redeemed in Christ, who hold to a "common confession" about Him (v. 16). How we conduct ourselves and live out that confession, inside and outside the church building, affects how Christian truth is perceived.

The Minister (Chaps. 4–6)

In the last half of the letter, Paul focuses on Timothy's personal life, encouraging him once again to be on guard against false doctrine, to discipline himself for godliness, and to pay close attention to the needs of the flock.

The Certainty of Apostasy

Wherever the light of the Gospel shines, the shadow of false doctrine lurks closely behind. That's why Timothy, and we, should not be surprised to see people "fall away" from the faith and embrace

---

4. Some commentators understand the word for *women* in verse 11 as referring to the wives of deacons rather than to a formal office of deaconness.

religions characterized by unbiblical extremes, such as Gnosticism, asceticism, and legalistic ritual (4:1–5).[5]

In order for Timothy to publicly confront such false teaching, he must immerse himself in sound doctrine, resist the lure of "worldly fables," and be self-disciplined (vv. 6–11). His personal holiness will make his ministry effective. Therefore, his youthfulness need not obscure his usefulness (v. 12).

Timothy is a gifted man. But giftedness must be accompanied by godliness. Paul urges Timothy not only to pay attention to his teaching but to himself as well (vv. 13–15). This combination helps communicate clearly the saving message of the Gospel (v. 16).

Caring for Those in God's Household

When the minister gives attention to his own spirit, he can more effectively care for others. So Paul turns now to the various groups of people in the church and Timothy's involvement in their lives.

He should approach older men with love, respect, and gentleness rather than with a harsh rebuke; younger men as brothers; older women as mothers; and younger women as sisters, "in all purity" (5:1–2). In verses 13–16, Paul advises Timothy on how to discern which widows should be supported financially by the church.

Turning to elders, particularly those who preach and teach, Paul writes that they should be fairly compensated for their service (vv. 17–18). Also, elders should never be irresponsibly accused of sin; at least two witnesses need to concur (vv. 19–20), and those charges should be handled without any favoritism or partiality (v. 21). Just as dangerous as hasty accusations are hasty appointments, which can result in unqualified leaders being placed in office. Paul is saying to take enough time in selecting leaders to recognize both strengths and weaknesses (vv. 24–25).

With all these needs, however, Timothy isn't to neglect his own health. He should apply whatever remedy is necessary for his own physical ailments (v. 23).

---

5. Gnostics taught that only the Spirit is good and matter is evil (for further information on Gnosticism, see chapter 10, "1 John: God's Life on Display"). This resulted in asceticism, which urged the avoidance of anything pleasurable to the body and sometimes led to an abusive self-deprivation. The Judaizers promoted strict observance of Jewish law for salvation.

Doctrine and Personal Integrity

Turning once again to the importance of sound doctrine, Paul points out that truth is upheld in the way we relate to one another in the body. Even the way slaves and masters now relate to one another in Christ can affect how readily onlookers embrace Christian truth (6:1–2). This truth, unfortunately, gets distorted when false teachers, leading out of their conceit, turn their attention to "controversial questions and disputes" and greedily divide a congregation (6:3–5).

Personal integrity *must* accompany doctrinal integrity. Spiritual leaders should be content with the necessities of life and not lust after wealth (vv. 6–10). Paul urges Timothy to flee worldly temptations and pursue the things of God (vv. 11–16), while at the same time urging those who are blessed with riches to see their wealth as a gift from God and a resource to help those in need (vv. 17–19).

Paul's final words serve to burn the importance of sound doctrine into Timothy's mind one more time:

> O Timothy, guard what has been entrusted to you, avoiding worldly and empty chatter and the opposing arguments of what is falsely called "knowledge"—which some have professed and thus gone astray from the faith.
> Grace be with you. (vv. 20–21)

The purity of the Gospel. The integrity of our hearts. The needs of our flock. All treasures worth guarding . . . and adventures worth taking.

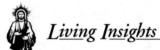 *Living Insights*

"Let's not go overboard on doctrine. Ministry, after all, is about caring for people."

Perhaps you've heard ministry defined this way. And perhaps you've wondered how we got the idea that ministry is either doctrine *or* caring for people? According to Paul, it's both!

In fact, a pastor who truly cares about his congregation will care about the teaching they receive. His heart will ache when people are misled by teaching that dishonors Christ. He will long to lead to freedom those who are in bondage to legalism. And he will labor long and hard to equip God's flock to defend themselves against wolves that prey on weak, underfed sheep.

How about the ministry in which you are involved? Does it balance doctrinal instruction with meeting the other needs of the flock?

_____

How could it be more balanced?

_____

_____

What's a first step you can take toward aligning your ministry more closely with the truths in 1 Timothy?

_____

_____

_____

Clearly and consistently teaching biblical truth. It's one of the most tangible ways to say "I care" to God's people.

Chapter 3

2 TIMOTHY: PAUL'S SWAN SONG

A Survey of 2 Timothy

By A.D. 67, four years after Paul wrote 1 Timothy, Christianity had become a stench in the nostrils of Rome. Christians had the audacity to refuse to acknowledge the emperor Nero as a god. To make matters worse, the egotistical ruler had convinced the populace that this "anti-imperial" sect deliberately set the great fire of A.D. 64, which destroyed half of Rome. Christians were now official enemies of the state, subject to public torture and execution.

The apostle Paul, caught up in the undertow of the swelling wave of persecution, now found himself in the courts of Rome, charged with "propagating a forbidden cult."[1] As if this opposition weren't enough, Paul also faced abandonment from within his own ranks.

> Fearing for their own lives, the Asian believers failed to support Paul after his arrest (1:15) and no one supported him at his first defense before the Imperial Court (4:16). Abandoned by almost everyone (4:10–11), the apostle found himself in circumstances very different from those of his first Roman imprisonment (Acts 28:16–31). At that time he was merely under house arrest, people could freely visit him, and he had the hope of release. Now he was in a cold Roman cell (4:13), regarded "as an evildoer" (2:9), and without hope of acquittal in spite of the success of his initial defense (4:6–8, 17–18).[2]

Shivering. Shrouded in the shadowy, earthy air of the underground Mamertine dungeon. Alone, except for Luke and a few other occasional visitors. Under these bleak conditions Paul once again—and for the last time—wrote to Timothy, his dear son in the faith, about the matters most pressing on his heart.

1. John Pollock, *The Apostle* (Wheaton, Ill.: Scripture Press Publications, Victor Books, 1969), p. 235.

2. Bruce Wilkinson and Kenneth Boa, *Talk Thru the Bible* (Nashville, Tenn.: Thomas Nelson Publishers, 1983), p. 434.

2 TIMOTHY

	Guard the Treasure!	Suffer Hardship!	Continue!	Preach the Word!
	Paul's greeting	Passing on the Truth	Last days	A solemn charge
	Timothy's life	Illustrations of the Truth	Evil people	Reason for the charge
	God's treasure	(Soldier, athlete, farmer, workman, vessel, servant)	Standing firm	Personal conclusion
	Our responsibility		Biblical basis	
		Suffering for the Truth	Spiritual examples	
	CHAPTER 1	CHAPTER 2	CHAPTER 3	CHAPTER 4
Perspective	The past	The present	The future	
Tone	Gratitude	Compassion	Warning	Command
Main Theme		Paul's passing of the ministry torch to Timothy and encouraging him to stay faithful in the midst of hardship		
Key Verse	"Guard, through the Holy Spirit who dwells in us, the treasure which has been entrusted to you." (1:14)	"Suffer hardship with me, as a good soldier of Christ Jesus." (2:3)	"You, however, continue in the things you have learned and become convinced of, knowing from whom you have learned them." (3:14)	"Preach the word; be ready in season and out of season; reprove, rebuke, exhort, with great patience and instruction." (4:2)

20

Inspired Last Words

Though 2 Timothy appears between 1 Timothy and Titus in the Bible, it was actually written four years after these letters, making it Paul's final epistle. Some have even described 2 Timothy as an inspired last will and testament in which Paul imparted "his final words of wisdom and encouragement to Timothy who [was] ministering in the midst of opposition and hardship in Ephesus."[3]

Colored by the imminence of Paul's execution, 2 Timothy is both emotional and urgent in tone.

Longing for Friends

Though Paul's trust in Christ was as strong as ever (1:8–12), his yearning for friends and his heartache over those who had abandoned him blow through the letter like a chill wind. He longed to see Timothy again (1:4) and asked him to come before the onset of winter (4:21). The mention of Luke's companionship and Paul's request that Timothy bring Mark (4:11) also reveal the apostle's need for the presence of dear friends and co-laborers.

Many had turned their backs on Paul (1:15; 4:10, 14–15), but he stood firm and "fought the good fight" (4:7). With the "time of [his] departure" near (v. 6), his only requests beyond close friends were his cloak to keep out the cold and his copies of the Scriptures (4:13).

Urgency about Ministry

There's more to 2 Timothy, though, than Paul's loneliness. The letter is full of instruction and encouragement to Timothy. Apparently, the heretical teaching Paul addressed in 1 Timothy had not subsided in Ephesus. It may, in fact, have become more widespread. So, out of the apostle's dark dungeon comes a light of help and hope, not only to Timothy personally, but to the church of his day . . . and ours.

Paul's letter resounds with urgent imperatives that suggest spiritual awareness and action: "kindle afresh" (1:6), "retain" (v. 13), "guard" (v. 14), "be strong" (2:1), "suffer" (v. 3), "be diligent" (v. 15), "flee . . . pursue" (v. 22), "realize" (3:1), "continue" (v. 14), "preach" (4:2), "be on guard" (v. 15).

Christian leaders all over the world minister every day in overwhelming circumstances. Second Timothy is for everyone tempted to throw in the towel. This letter reminds us that the Gospel is

3. Wilkinson and Boa, *Talk Thru the Bible*, p. 432.

worth the battle, and that God is faithful to equip us, strengthen us, and uphold the truth of His Word.

Structure of 2 Timothy

One way to organize 2 Timothy is by the key imperative statements in each chapter: "Guard . . . the treasure" (1:14), "suffer hardship" (2:3), "continue in the things you have learned" (3:14), "preach the word" (4:2).

"Guard the Treasure!" (Chap. 1)

In the first chapter, Paul encourages his "beloved son" to persevere in his present ministry by looking back on his spiritual heritage.

A Family Heritage of Faith

After offering thanksgiving for Timothy (1:3) and expressing sadness that the two are apart (v. 4), Paul reminds the young leader of his Christian heritage (v. 5).

Timothy probably needed this reminder. He might have been wondering if the Gospel could overcome, or even withstand, the storm of heresy raging through Asia Minor. He might even have wondered if the Gospel was worth fighting for. It was, Paul reassures him. Through the message of Christ, God has made Timothy a man of noticeable faith and has saved three generations of his family. What an encouragement this must have been for him to stay in the battle for truth.

There's good reason to believe that Timothy might have become discouraged, even lax, in his ministry. For Paul reminds him to

> kindle afresh the gift of God which is in you through the laying on of my hands. For God has not given us a spirit of timidity, but of power and love and discipline. (vv. 6–7)

Timothy's giftedness—his God-given ability for ministry—had been confirmed at his ordination (laying on of hands). But now the gifts needed stirring up. His self-discipline may have waned in study and prayer. He may have been preaching, teaching, and contending for the faith with diminished fervor. It was time to fan the dying embers of God's gifts into full flame.

Suffering and Standing for the Gospel

Timothy might even have been embarrassed about associating

himself with the cause of Christ, since it was so opposed by society; further, his own mentor, Paul, was in prison. But Paul admonishes his friend, "Do not be ashamed of the testimony of our Lord or of me His prisoner, but join with me in suffering for the gospel according to the power of God" (v. 8).[4]

Suffering, Paul explains, may last for a time in this life, but we suffer for the truth of an eternal message—a God who loved and chose a people for Himself before time, sent His Son to die for them, and gave them eternal life (vv. 9–12).

No, the Gospel is nothing to be ashamed of. It constitutes "sound words" that need to be preserved and taught (v. 13). The Gospel is a treasure of truth which has been entrusted to us. As Paul tells Timothy, "Guard, through the Holy Spirit who dwells in us, the treasure" (v. 14).

Chapter 1 closes with Paul's mention of those who had deserted him (v. 15) and his blessings on Onesiphorus, who served Christ well and encouraged Paul in his imprisonment (vv. 16–18).

"Suffer Hardship!" (Chap. 2)

In light of Onesiphorus' positive model, Paul urges Timothy to "be strong in the grace that is in Christ Jesus" (2:1). The grace Paul speaks of "was a divine 'gift' (grace, *charis*), found only in Christ."[5] Therefore, only clothed in Christ's strength could Timothy pass on "the things which [he had] heard from [Paul] in the presence of many witnesses" (v. 2). It is Christ's faithfulness, working through us, that enables the Gospel to advance.

Enduring Hardship

Empowered by Christ, Timothy can stay at the hard work of declaring the Gospel, even if it means suffering. Like a single-minded soldier, a winning athlete, and a hard-working farmer, Timothy will have to invest his energy and endure hardship to serve the Gospel properly (vv. 3–7).

It is not just for a message but for a person that Timothy

---

4. Suffering is part and parcel of standing for the Gospel. It is, in fact, as Scripture states elsewhere, a privilege to identify with Christ in His sufferings (Matt. 5:11–12; Acts 5:41; Phil. 3:10). And it is in our suffering, as it was with Christ's suffering, that the power of God is made manifest.

5. A. Duane Litfin, "2 Timothy," in *The Bible Knowledge Commentary*, New Testament edition, ed. John F. Walvoord and Roy B. Zuck (Wheaton, Ill.: Scripture Press Publications, Victor Books, 1983), p. 752.

endures—Jesus Christ Himself (v. 8). It is He, says Paul, who is the source and substance of "my gospel" and the reason for his suffering. Though Paul is chained, Christ's Gospel cannot be. Therefore, if Paul's imprisonment can advance the Gospel, he is willing to endure it (v. 10).

Paul's reflecting on Christ brings to his mind a "trustworthy statement," possibly a baptism hymn or creed of the day:

> It is a trustworthy statement:
> For if we died with Him, we will also live with
>   Him;
> If we endure, we will also reign with Him;
> If we deny Him, He also will deny us;
> If we are faithless, He remains faithful, for He
>   cannot deny Himself. (vv. 11–13)

A Workman Approved by God

Timothy is to remind others of this creed and all the truth it represents (v. 14). Reminiscent of his first letter, Paul urges his young friend to avoid divisive discussion and instead focus on "accurately handling the word of truth" (vv. 15–17).

Two who had poisoned the church with divisive teaching were Hymenaeus and Philetus. They were apparently promoting the Gnostic idea that the resurrection was purely spiritual, having "occurred at conversion or baptism."[6] This "spirit-only" resurrection, denying a bodily resurrection, led to a disregard for the body, often resulting in either physical self-abuse or licentious living.

This fallacious teaching "upset the faith of some," but despite its destructive power, Timothy is grounded in something stronger. As Paul reaffirms,

> Nevertheless, the firm foundation of God stands,
> having this seal, "The Lord knows those who are
> His," and, "Everyone who names the name of the
> Lord is to abstain from wickedness." (2:19)

These words of Paul, which draw upon and reflect other Scripture passages (see Num. 16:5; Acts 2:21; Rom. 10:13), point out that the permanence and power of the church rest on God's choice

---

6. Litfin, "2 Timothy," p. 754.

24

and ownership of her. So, in spite of the proliferation of heresy, God's true church will endure. Our calling in light of that sureness is to live in a way that honors Him.

The visible church on earth, however, has always been and will continue to be a mixture of true believers (gold and silver vessels, 2 Tim. 2:20) and false teachers (vessels of wood and earthenware). Those who cleanse themselves (forsake false teaching) will be vessels of honor used in the service of our Master.

Chapter 2 closes with Paul's exhortation to Timothy to pursue godliness and avoid evil, once again emphasizing the need to shun divisive quarrels (vv. 22–23). Instead, Timothy should gently correct those who oppose the truth, in the hope that they will repent and escape "the snare of the devil, having been held captive by him to do his will" (vv. 24–26).

"Continue!" (Chap. 3)

Speaking of the devil, Paul now shifts to what Timothy can expect in the future "last days."

The Certainty of False Teaching

One would think that Paul might try to encourage Timothy by telling him things would get better. But Paul doesn't paint a false picture of the future. Instead, he prepares Timothy for the degeneration of society (3:1–5) and the fact that false teachers will always be lurking around the church (vv. 6–7).

Paul, however, doesn't end on this depressing note. As he has assured Timothy throughout the letter, God has the final word. Just as Jannes and Jambres, who sought to emulate divine power through magic in Moses' day (compare Exod. 7:11), were exposed as frauds before God's power (2 Tim. 3:8), so false teachers will be exposed by the light of God's truth (v. 9).

"Continue in the Things You Have Learned"

In light of the inevitability of false teachers (v. 13), Timothy is to "continue in the things you have learned and become convinced of" (v. 14). This would include Paul's teaching of the Gospel, his Christian character, his example of perseverance in suffering (vv. 10–12), as well as the Scriptures (v. 15). The "sacred writings" Timothy has been exposed to since childhood contain the true message of salvation. They led him to salvation, and they will reveal

Christ's redemption to those who follow his teaching.

The Scriptures—Old Testament and New—are the key to godly living, since God inspired (breathed out) the words Himself (v. 16). Through His Word, we become "adequate" for the challenges ahead and "equipped for every good work" (v. 17).

"Preach the Word!" (Chap. 4)

Given Paul's exalted view of God's Word, as well as Timothy's scriptural heritage, it's no surprise that the apostle's next words are a solemn charge to Timothy to "preach the word; be ready in season and out of season; reprove, rebuke, exhort, with great patience and instruction" (4:1–2).

Confronting False Doctrine

Unfortunately, "the time will come when" people will not be interested in or even tolerate sound doctrine and truth (vv. 3–4). In contrast to those so willing to embrace and advance false doctrine, Timothy must "be sober in all things, endure hardship, do the work of an evangelist, fulfill your ministry" (v. 5).

Paul has "fought the good fight" (v. 7). He is ready to depart and be with the Lord. And young Timothy, into whom the apostle has poured his life, must carry on the fight for the Gospel of grace.

Closing Words to a Close Friend

"Make every effort to come to me soon" (v. 9). We can almost see Paul pause after writing these words and speak them out loud. Perhaps they fluttered the flame of his candle, resonated softly in his stone cell, then dissolved in the darkness.

Most of his coworkers have either abandoned him or are involved in ministry elsewhere (v. 10). One, Alexander, actively did him harm, and Paul warns Timothy to be on guard against him (vv. 14–15). Only Luke, the loyal physician, remains with Paul now (v. 11).

So Paul longs to see Timothy, whom he asks to bring a few personal treasures—a cloak to warm his body and the Scriptures to warm his soul. He even asks Timothy to bring Mark, who had failed Paul earlier in his ministry. Now, though, Mark has matured and become "useful" (vv. 11, 13).

The Lord, however, has not abandoned Paul. He stands by and strengthens him and will "bring [him] safely to His heavenly kingdom; to Him be the glory forever and ever. Amen" (vv. 17–18).

In closing, Paul sends greetings from himself and other believers and urges Timothy to "come before winter" (v. 21). Before the unbearable cold. Before the final sentencing. Before the executioner's blade ends Paul's earthly sojourn and sends him home. Home at last.

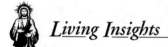 ## *Living Insights*

Ministry, any kind of ministry, is difficult. Especially if we're serious about our faith and committed to a true and clear presentation of the Gospel. "All who desire to live godly in Christ Jesus," said Paul, "will be persecuted" (2 Tim. 3:12).

Has standing up for Christ and His Gospel brought some hardship, conflict, or persecution into your life?

_____

_____

What encouragement can you garner from 2 Timothy to stay on course?

_____

_____

_____

How does the value of Christ's suffering—the salvation it accomplished, the honor it brought His Father, etc.—encourage you about the value of your own hardship?

_____

_____

_____

Hardship is part of the Christian life. But so are union with Christ, the presence of His Spirit, and joyful fellowship with other Christians. And they last a lot longer than hardship—forever, in fact. So keep standing strong. And know that our Lord stands with you. Now and forever.

Chapter 4

TITUS: PLAIN TALK
FOR PASTORS

A Survey of Titus

Paul and Timothy. Having read about the special bond of love
and friendship between these two men in 1 and 2 Timothy,
one might assume that Timothy was Paul's one and only protégé.
But he wasn't. Paul had another "son" in the faith.

His name was Titus. Though not as well-known as Timothy,
Titus was no less important to Paul's ministry and the spread of the
Gospel. In fact, as a converted Gentile who was not "compelled to
be circumcised" for salvation by the church leaders (see Gal. 2:3),
Titus became a living reminder of salvation by faith alone—and of
God's opening up of His kingdom not only to the Jews but to every
nation, tribe, and tongue.

Titus eventually proved himself a capable and faithful minister;
so, like Timothy, he was left in charge of a significant ministry. This
ministry, though, was full of problems and challenges, and Titus
needed the input of his mentor.

Let's take a look at Titus, then, the last of the pastoral epistles,
and consider Paul's straightforward advice about leading in the local
church.

Paul and Titus: Co-laborers for Christ

Though never mentioned in the historical book of Acts, Titus
is referred to thirteen times in Paul's epistles. He was, no doubt,
one of Paul's closest and most trusted companions. Authors Bruce
Wilkinson and Kenneth Boa trace their ministry together.

> This convert of Paul ("my true son in *our* common
> faith," 1:4) was probably from Syrian Antioch, if he
> was one of the disciples of Acts 11:26. Paul brought
> this uncircumcised Greek believer to Jerusalem
> (Gal. 2:3) where he became a test case on the matter
> of Gentiles and liberty from the Law. Years later
> when Paul set out from Antioch on his third mis-
> sionary journey (Acts 18:22), Titus must have

28

TITUS

	Taking Charge	Giving Advice	Doing Right
	Elders Rebellious people	Older men and women Young women and men Titus and all leaders Slaves and masters	What to do What not to do
	CHAPTER 1	*CHAPTER 2*	*CHAPTER 3*
People	Elders Enemies	Specific groups	Christians in general
Issue	Setting up the right leadership	Instruction for particular people	Attitude and conduct toward good and bad
A Church	... in good order *(1:5)*	... with good doctrine *(2:1)*	... of good deeds *(3:1)*
Main Theme	Titus' role in encouraging right living through sound doctrine		
Key Verses	1:5; 2:10b; 3:8		

accompanied him because he was sent by the apostle to Corinth on three occasions during that time (see 2 Cor. 2:12–13; 7:5–7, 13–15; 8:6, 16–24). He is not mentioned again until Paul leaves him in Crete to carry on the work (1:5). He was with Paul during his second Roman imprisonment but left to go to Dalmatia (2 Tim. 4:10), possibly on an evangelistic mission. Paul spoke of this reliable and gifted associate as his "brother" (2 Cor. 2:13), his "partner and fellow worker" (2 Cor. 8:23), and his "son" (1:4). He lauded Titus' character and conduct in Second Corinthians 7:13–15; 8:16–17.[1]

Sometime after Paul's release from his first Roman imprisonment, he spread the Gospel on the island of Crete[2] and left Titus there to finish the work of organizing the churches. The apostle may have written to Titus from Corinth, possibly on his way to Spain. Paul later wrote 2 Timothy during his second imprisonment in Rome.

Crete: A Tough Place to Minister

"Cretans are always liars, evil beasts, lazy gluttons" (1:12). How would you like that slogan for your home town? Unfortunately, this saying wasn't invented by some tourist who had a bad stay in Crete; it originated with Epimenides, a poet who was a native of Knossos, Crete, in the sixth century B.C.[3]

Things apparently hadn't improved much by Paul's day. Although the light of the church was helping some in Crete find their way out of darkness, the population was still characterized by its excessive immorality. The Cretans were the inspiration behind the word *kretizein*, which means to "play the liar."[4]

Such immorality may be partly attributable to Crete's location. Seafaring traffic from around the world stopped at this island in the

1. Bruce Wilkinson and Kenneth Boa, *Talk Thru the Bible* (Nashville, Tenn.: Thomas Nelson Publishers, 1983), p. 438.

2. We don't know for sure if Paul founded the church in Crete. Jews from Crete were present at Pentecost, so they may have taken the Gospel back to their land (see Acts 2:11).

3. D. Edmond Hiebert, note on Titus 1:12, in *The NIV Study Bible*, ed. Kenneth L. Barker and others (Grand Rapids, Mich.: Zondervan Bible Publishers, 1985), p. 1851.

4. Merrill F. Unger, *Unger's Bible Dictionary*, 3d ed. (Chicago, Ill.: Moody Press, 1966), p. 227.

middle of the Mediterranean, southeast of Greece. No doubt it bustled regularly with sea-weary sailors on shore leave.

Stylistic Comparison to 1 and 2 Timothy

The letter to Titus was written about the same time as 1 Timothy, though it appears last in biblical order. Second Timothy was Paul's last letter.

Like 1 and 2 Timothy, Titus was written to help one of Paul's representatives with administrative and doctrinal matters in the local church. In his letter to Titus, however, Paul didn't emphasize doctrine as much as he did in 1 and 2 Timothy. Wilkinson and Boa point out that

> Titus and First Timothy are similar in date, circumstances, and purposes. Both give instructions on qualifications for leadership, how to deal with false teaching, and the need for sound doctrine and behavior. Both contain encouragement and exhortation to Paul's representatives, but Titus is briefer, more official, and less personal than First Timothy. The situation at Ephesus required a stronger emphasis on sound doctrine, while that at Crete required more concentration on conduct. Even so, Titus offers three excellent summaries of Christian theology (1:1–4; 2:11–14; 3:4–7), and the last two are among the most sublime New Testament portraits of the grace of God.[5]

Structure of Titus

Titus is easy to read, and we can outline it according to the three chapter divisions. In chapter 1, Paul addresses the need for Titus to take charge in Crete by appointing elders and opposing false teachers. Chapter 2 deals with advising various groups in the church on how to live. Chapter 3 emphasizes the importance of living out the truth of the Christian life by doing good works.

5. Wilkinson and Boa, *Talk Thru the Bible*, p. 440.

Taking Charge (Chap. 1)

In a theologically rich greeting, Paul introduces himself as an apostle and bondservant of Christ, a minister of the life-giving Gospel, and calls Titus his "true child in a common faith" (1:1–4). Then he reminds Titus of his duties in Crete:

> For this reason I left you in Crete, that you would set in order what remains and appoint elders in every city as I directed you. (1:5)

If the infant church in Crete is to grow up, it needs structure and guidance. The task of providing these has fallen to Titus. And Paul's endorsement of and charge to Titus provides this young leader with the authority and, no doubt, the encouragement to perform his duties.

Appointing Elders

Titus' first order of business is to assign capable men to spiritual oversight of the church. The qualifications for these leaders, outlined in verses 6–9, are essentially the same as those listed in 1 Timothy 3:2–7: blameless behavior in personal, public, family, and church life. Does this mean that only those who have reached a state of sinless perfection can serve as elders? Not at all. Commentator Philip H. Towner explains that *blamelessness*

> is more a measure of wholeness and balance than of perfection. The code examines all dimensions of life for evidence of the Spirit's influence in each part. This kind of balanced "reading" means development toward maturity is under way. And Paul felt that "whole" believers were best suited for church leadership.[6]

Opposing False Teachers

Paul's last item on the list of qualifications for elder—that he must know the Word well enough to uphold sound doctrine and refute falsehood (Titus 1:9)—leads him naturally into an exposure of the false teachers who have arisen in the Cretan church.

---

6. Philip H. Towner, *1–2 Timothy and Titus*, The IVP New Testament Commentary Series (Downers Grove, Ill.: InterVarsity Press, 1994), p. 229.

They are "rebellious men, empty talkers and deceivers, especially those of the circumcision" (v. 10). In other words, they openly defy the Gospel and Paul's authority, they engage in speculation rather than truth, and they willfully lead others astray. "Those of the circumcision" gives us a clue that Jews who demanded adherence to ceremonial law are involved.

So, how should the church respond? Should it let false teachers have their say? Should it give the opposing view "equal time?" No way! They "must be silenced," says Paul (v. 11), because their teaching is affecting the life of the church ("upsetting whole families"). Their corrupt message, you see, flows from corrupt motives ("sordid gain"). These false teachers are more interested in making money than ministering to people.

In verse 12 Paul quotes the poet Epimenides, who was also widely believed to have been a religious prophet. The poet's unflattering assessment of his own countrymen, that they are "liars, evil beasts, lazy gluttons," has been embodied in Titus' day in the deceitful, predatory, and self-serving false teachers.

These teachers must be reproved and, if possible, restored to the true faith (v. 13), so that they may not again be led astray by "Jewish myths and commandments of men who turn away from the truth" (v. 14).

The false teachers, like the Pharisees in Jesus' day, imagined they were pure because of their external religious observances. They were, however, "defiled and unbelieving" (v. 15), claiming to know God but cutting themselves off from true grace and true good works (vv. 15–16).

Advising Others (Chap. 2)

Paul now shifts from the protection of sound doctrine to the practice of sound doctrine. This connection between belief and behavior, as Towner explains, must be grasped by all Christians if we're to be in the world but not of the world.

> The fact of the matter is that the Christian faith intends full engagement in the world. Certainly the origin of this new life is otherworldly. Certainly Christian values are not those of the world. Certainly Christian hope takes us beyond this world. But it is in this world that God has called Christians to live, and it is this world's inhabitants that

Christians must reach with the gospel. Engagement of this kind requires Christian credibility and participation in the life of the world.[7]

In Paul's instructions to Titus about how to teach various people, the apostle shows the importance of bearing fruit for Christ—regardless of our age, gender, occupation, or any other classification. When we come to faith, Christ may not ask us to alter our situation. But He does call us to live differently in whatever environment we find ourselves.

Instructions for Various Groups

Older men should manifest the marks of spiritual and emotional maturity (2:2). Older women are to behave reverently and respectfully, avoiding gossip and drunkenness (v. 3). They should channel their energy into teaching younger women how to love their families and live godly lives (vv. 4–5). As for younger men, they are to display sensibility ("be self-controlled" in the NIV, v. 6).

Titus, who would probably have qualified as a "young man," is to be a living example of his teaching. He is to keep his life and doctrine pure and "beyond reproach" so that those who would desire to slander the Christian faith would be shamed into silence (vv. 7–8).

Finally, rather than urging Christian slaves to revolt, Titus must encourage them to submit to their masters, work hard to please them, avoid arguing with them, and resist stealing from them (vv. 9–10a). They must work in good faith "so that in every way they will make the teaching about God our Savior attractive" (v. 10b NIV).

The Reason for the Instructions

Are these instructions merely based on empty moralism? No, says Paul. We're to live this way because

> the grace of God has appeared, bringing salvation to all men, instructing us to deny ungodliness and worldly desires and to live sensibly, righteously and godly in the present age, looking for the blessed hope and the appearing of the glory of our great God and Savior, Christ Jesus, who gave Himself for us to

7. Towner, *1–2 Timothy and Titus*, pp. 233–34.

redeem us from every lawless deed, and to purify for Himself a people for His own possession, zealous for good deeds. (vv. 11–14)

Jesus saved us, not only so we would belong to Him, but also so we would *live like we belong to Him*. Titus, and all teachers, should teach "these things" (v. 15).

Doing Right (Chap. 3)

Having instructed Titus on how to instruct various groups of people to behave, Paul now turns to the church's responsibility toward civil authorities and all people in general.

Being Good Citizens

Christians are to respect and obey the civil authorities and do good to "all men" (3:1–2). They should "be an influence for good in the community in every way, demonstrating the loveliness of Christ to all through courteous and gracious behavior."[8]

Since Christ has saved us, our old, selfish ways of relating to people (v. 3) need not control us. Through the Holy Spirit, we can live in a way that honors Him. As in 2:11–14, Paul here gives a beautiful capsulation of the work of salvation and sanctification God so graciously provides us.

> When the kindness of God our Savior and His love for mankind appeared, He saved us, not on the basis of deeds which we have done in righteousness, but according to His mercy, by the washing of regeneration and renewing by the Holy Spirit, whom He poured out upon us richly through Jesus Christ our Savior, so that being justified by His grace we would be made heirs according to the hope of eternal life. (3:4–7)

In light of all that God has done for us, Titus is to promote good deeds among fellow Christians, because they profit everyone (v. 8). Divisive teachings and controversies, however, don't accomplish

---

8. A. Duane Litfin, "Titus," in *The Bible Knowledge Commentary*, New Testament edition, ed. John F. Walvoord and Roy B. Zuck (Wheaton, Ill.: Scripture Press Publications, Victor Books, 1983), p. 766.

anything good, so Titus should avoid them (v. 9). Those promoting the latter should be confronted and, if necessary, excommunicated (vv. 10–11).

Personal Matters

In Paul's closing remarks, we're reminded that his instruction by mail to Titus is rooted in their personal relationship. Paul planned to send others to spell Titus in Crete so the two could meet in Nicopolis, on the Adriatic coast of Greece, for the winter (v. 12).

After sending greetings from others and a final reminder of the importance of "good deeds" (vv. 13–14), Paul closes with a revealing wish: "Grace be with you all." The plural indicates that Paul's instructions are meant for more than just Titus. They are meant for the entire church. Then . . . and now.

 Living Insights

And so ends our study of the pastoral epistles—1 and 2 Timothy and Titus. With so much crucial information about the local church given in these letters, it's worth stopping to soak in some of it.

Based on these three letters, how would you summarize the main priority of pastors and elders?

_____

_____

_____

What's the best way to teach our congregations to recognize false teaching?

_____

_____

_____

What do Paul's strong words against false teachers, such as the Judaizers, tell you about the importance of God's grace in Christian teaching?

_____

_____

_____

What do Paul's relationships with Timothy and Titus tell you about the need for leaders to avoid isolation and, instead, minister with and to others and pass on the treasure of Christ?

_____

_____

_____

Finally, what do these letters tell you about the importance of understanding what Christ has done for us before we can do anything for Him?

_____

_____

_____

Now, is your church on track?

Chapter 5

PHILEMON: AN APPEAL FOR GRACE AND FORGIVENESS

A Survey of Philemon

Of the thirteen letters Paul wrote in the New Testament, Philemon is the shortest—only twenty-five verses. It's like a postcard, really. But don't let the length deceive you. Though short in size, it's long on truth.

Writing from Rome, Paul addressed a friend of his in the Colossian church named Philemon. Paul's purpose wasn't to confront a heresy or straighten out a doctrinal confusion. Instead, with a warm, personal tone, he wrote to restore a broken relationship. He appealed to Philemon to welcome back his runaway slave, Onesimus, who had become a Christian through Paul's ministry.

Between the lines of this picture postcard of forgiveness is a message for us all—a message about second chances and showing mercy. A message about equality in Christ and the power of the Gospel to transcend social boundaries. A message about grace.

The Historical Background

As with any correspondence, Paul's letter to Philemon bears the imprint of the context in which it was written.

Flight to Freedom

Paul was living in Rome under house arrest, awaiting a trial before Caesar. Though in chains, he was free to proclaim Christ to all who came to him (Acts 28:16–31), including the soldiers who guarded him—and a certain young slave named Onesimus.

Onesimus was one of about sixty million slaves who shouldered the weight of the Roman Empire. Though the lot of slaves has never been something to envy, in Rome it could be particularly inhumane, as William Barclay describes.

This chapter has been adapted from "A Postcard to Philemon," in the study guide *New Testament Postcards*, coauthored by Ken Gire and Bryce Klabunde, from the Bible-teaching ministry of Charles R. Swindoll (Anaheim, Calif.: Insight for Living, 1996).

PHILEMON

Greeting (Verses 1–3) | Conclusion (Verses 21–25)

	Paul's Commendation	Paul's Request	Paul's Promise
	VERSES 4–7	On the basis of the slave's conversion *(verses 8–11)* On the basis of the slave owner's friendship *(verses 12–17)* *VERSES 8–17*	*VERSES 18–21*
Tone	Praise	Plea	Promise
Direction	Looking back	Looking within	Looking beyond
Central Statement	*"I thank my God always . . ."* (v. 4)	*"I appeal to you . . ."* (v. 10)	*"I will repay it . . ."* (v. 19)
Main Theme	Forgiving and accepting one another as brothers and sisters in Christ		
Key Verses	Verses 10–11, 15–18		

39

A slave was not a person; he was a living tool. A master had absolute power over his slaves. "He can box their ears or condemn them to hard labor— making them, for instance, work in chains upon his lands in the country, or in a sort of prison-factory. Or, he may punish them with blows of the rod, the lash or the knot; he can brand them upon the forehead, if they are thieves or runaways, or, in the end, if they prove irreclaimable, he can crucify them."[1]

With only a life shaped by someone else's whims to look forward to, is it any wonder that Onesimus made a wild grasp for freedom? As a fugitive slave, however, he was in constant danger of being found out. His only hope for survival was to flee to Rome and lose himself in the faceless sea of people.

Finding the Ultimate Freedom

Before he ran away from Philemon, Onesimus appears to have stolen something from his master, possibly to finance his flight (Philem. 18). So not only was he a fugitive, he was a thief—a candidate for branding (or worse) if he was caught and returned. Freedom would not have felt very free with thoughts like that binding his every move.

Fortunately, God had a freedom waiting for him that was higher and wider than anything of which he had ever dreamed of.

The Lord arranged to bring Onesimus into contact with Paul, who introduced him to the Savior. When Onesimus reached out in faith, his shackles of fear and shame dropped to the ground. In Christ, the fugitive found forgiveness. Now he was *really* free.

Liberty in Christ, however, doesn't mean being absolved from all earthly debts and responsibilities. Onesimus had been made righteous in Christ's eyes, but Paul knew that he now needed to make things right with Philemon. Returning to his master, however, meant dealing with two risky issues:

- First, there was the matter of property loss. When Onesimus ran away, he cost Philemon the amount of the item he had

---

1. William Barclay, *The Letters to Timothy, Titus, and Philemon*, rev. ed., The Daily Study Bible series (Philadelphia, Pa.: Westminster Press, 1975), p. 270.

stolen as well as the price his master had originally paid for him. So Onesimus left behind not only a fractured relationship but an unresolved debt.

- Second, there was the matter of an angry master. Christ had forgiven Onesimus . . . but would Philemon? Could the Christian master accept the repentant slave as a brother in the faith? It was the ultimate test of Christian fellowship and the power of the Gospel to break down social walls.

With these two issues on the table, Paul sat down to write a note for Onesimus to hand deliver to Philemon.

The Contents of Paul's Postcard

As we look at the text of Paul's postcard, four divisions emerge: a greeting, a commendation, a request, and a promise.

Greeting (vv. 1–3)

Paul begins his note with a humble and affectionate salutation.

> Paul, a prisoner of Christ Jesus, and Timothy our brother,
> To Philemon our beloved brother and fellow worker, and to Apphia our sister, and to Archippus our fellow soldier, and to the church in your house: Grace to you and peace from God our Father and the Lord Jesus Christ. (vv. 1–3)

Unpretentiously, Paul refers to himself as "a prisoner of Christ Jesus" rather than an apostle. He has devoted his life to Christ, as has Philemon—who was apparently one of Paul's converts living in Colossae.[2] Owning a home spacious enough to house the church and owning at least one slave, Philemon was probably a man of some means. Apphia (possibly his wife) and Archippus (possibly his son) shared in the ministry.

Paul asks God to show "grace" and "peace" to Philemon. Both words strengthen his plea. As Paul appeals to God to show grace

2. "He appears to have been a resident of Colossae, since his slave Onesimus is described in the Colossian letter as 'one of you' (4:9)." Curtis Vaughan, *Colossians and Philemon*, The Bible Study Commentary Series (Grand Rapids, Mich.: Zondervan Publishing House, Lamplighter Books, 1980), p. 123.

and peace to Philemon, so he will ask his friend to show a spirit of grace and peace to Onesimus.

Commendation (vv. 4–7)

Before he lays out his request, Paul expresses his gratitude for Philemon.

> I thank my God always, making mention of you in my prayers, because I hear of your love and of the faith which you have toward the Lord Jesus and toward all the saints; and I pray that the fellowship of your faith may become effective through the knowledge of every good thing which is in you for Christ's sake. For I have come to have much joy and comfort in your love, because the hearts of the saints have been refreshed through you, brother. (vv. 4–7)

An expert craftsman of letters, Paul builds a base of good rapport with Philemon before raising the delicate subject of Onesimus. He wastes not one word on flattery. His purpose is to encourage his brother in Christ and, at the same time, call him to a high moral standard—a standard Philemon has already been displaying in his refreshing spirit of love.

Request (vv. 8–17)

Without pulling rank or issuing orders, Paul now appeals to Philemon on the basis of love:

> Therefore, though I have enough confidence in Christ to order you to do what is proper, yet for love's sake I rather appeal to you—since I am such a person as Paul, the aged, and now also a prisoner of Christ Jesus—I appeal to you for my child Onesimus, whom I have begotten in my imprisonment. (vv. 8–10)

Onesimus. For Philemon, that name leaves the bitter aftertaste of disloyalty and desertion. Paul mentions it here for the first time, wisely sweetening the word with the phrase, "my child, whom I have begotten in my imprisonment."

In verse 11, Paul—using a play on the meaning of Onesimus' name, "Useful, Profitable"—explains the radical change in Onesimus' life as a result of his new birth in Christ:

who formerly was useless to you, but now is useful both to you and to me.

The one picture Philemon had in his mind was of the useless Onesimus of the past—a runaway and a thief. A more recent photo, however, which Paul reveals in the following verses, shows a useful Onesimus—a minister and a partner.

> I have sent him back to you in person, that is, send-ing my very heart, whom I wished to keep with me, so that on your behalf he might minister to me in my imprisonment for the gospel; but without your consent I did not want to do anything, so that your goodness would not be, in effect, by compulsion but of your own free will. For perhaps he was for this reason separated from you for a while, that you would have him back forever, no longer as a slave, but more than a slave, a beloved brother,[3] especially to me, but how much more to you, both in the flesh and in the Lord. If then you regard me a partner, accept him as you would me. (vv. 12–17)

In a legal sense, Paul's appeal is based on an advocacy clause in Roman law. Runaway slaves could return to their masters and be protected if they first went to their master's friend and secured support for their cause. The friend became an advocate, or mediator, who appealed to the slave's owner for grace and understanding. There were even some instances where the master not only accepted the slave back but adopted the slave into his family.[4]

In a spiritual sense, though, Paul's appeal is based on a much higher principle than Roman law: our unity in Christ. One commentator has observed,

> Here is a living example of Paul's statement that "there is neither Jew nor Greek, slave nor free, male nor female, for you are all one in Christ Jesus" (Gal. 3:28). It was in this oneness that Paul sought a

---

3. Notice that Paul called Philemon his beloved brother in verse 1—a subtle and quiet way of emphasizing their equality in Christ.

4. See J. Sidlow Baxter, "The Pastoral Epistles," in *Explore the Book*, one-volume ed. (Grand Rapids, Mich.: Zondervan Publishing House, Academie Books, 1966), pp. 253–54.

solution to the problem presented by the relationship of Onesimus to Philemon.[5]

Some have criticized Paul for not openly denouncing slavery when he had the opportunity. However, he does more than campaign for social reform; he campaigns for *heart* reform.

> Paul's approach . . . is not to attempt to abolish slavery as an institution but to call Christians to live out the implications of their common status as members of the redeemed community. Thus he sowed the seeds for a "spiritual"—rather than bloody—revolution.[6]

By asking Philemon to receive Onesimus "no longer as a slave, but more than a slave, a beloved brother" (v. 16), Paul essentially disables the institution of slavery at its core. Slavery can't exist in the presence of true Christian love.

Promise (vv. 18–25)

Nobody asked for fewer favors than Paul did. But now he asks for one, not so much for his sake, but for Onesimus' and Christ's and the church's sake. Paul even goes so far as to offer his own wallet on behalf of Onesimus:

> But if he has wronged you in any way or owes you anything, charge that to my account; I, Paul, am writing this with my own hand, I will repay it (not to mention to you that you owe to me even your own self as well). Yes, brother, let me benefit from you in the Lord; refresh my heart in Christ. (vv. 18–20)

Paul uses another subtle play on words in verse 20. *Benefit* also keys off Onesimus' name ("Profitable"), so Paul is saying, "I am benefiting you by sending Onesimus, all debts paid. Now let me, in return, be benefited by your willingness to forgive him."

Then, in verses 21–24, Paul signs off with a word of confidence

---

5. Arthur A. Rupprecht, "Philemon," in *The Expositor's Bible Commentary*, gen. ed. Frank E. Gaebelein (Grand Rapids, Mich.: Zondervan Publishing House, Regency Reference Library, 1978), vol. 11, p. 457.

6. William J. Moulder, "Onesimus," in *The International Standard Bible Encyclopedia*, gen. ed. Geoffrey W. Bromiley (Grand Rapids, Mich.: William B. Eerdmans Publishing Co., 1986), vol. 3, p. 604.

that Philemon will do the right thing.[7] Then he sends the greetings of several other believers who are with him in Rome. As a postscript, he leaves Philemon with this gentle benediction:

> The grace of the Lord Jesus Christ be with your spirit. (v. 25)

Grace. Slave or free, poor or rich, weak or powerful—Christ's grace levels the field so anyone who accepts it can enter into God's kingdom. With such a gift given to us, Paul would say today, how can we not extend it to others?

Living Insights

This ancient postcard to Philemon has a present-day postmark, with our names on the forwarding address. Let's look at some of the ways it applies to us.

1. *Every Christian was once a fugitive.* Enslaved to sin through Adam's fall, we ran from God, following our own paths instead of His (see Isa. 53:6).

2. *Our guilt was great and our penalty was severe.* Like Onesimus, we lived in fear of being found out. Guilt tormented our souls, and no matter where we ran, the grim sentence of death hung over our heads.

3. *Grace allowed us the right of appeal.* Pleading our case was our Advocate, Jesus Christ, who stood before the Judge and mediated on our behalf (see 1 Tim. 2:5).

4. *Christ said, "Charge that to My account!"* With His blood, He paid the debt we owe the Father for our sins (see Col. 2:13–14). We've been set free! And more than that, we've been embraced by the Father's love and adopted into His family (see Gal. 4:4–7).

Wow! That's grace.

How fully have you received God's grace? Do you feel the roominess in it, the welcome of it? Do you know in your heart that you're His child, His friend, and a slave no more?

---

7. Though history does not clearly reveal Philemon's response to Paul's letter, it does present us with an interesting possibility. Years later, the early church father Ignatius referred to a bishop of Ephesus named Onesimus—and Ignatius used the same play on words that Paul did with Onesimus' name. So the runaway slave, born anew by Christ's grace and nurtured by Philemon's forgiveness, may have become a great leader of the church. If this is true, he may also have been instrumental in getting this letter of Paul's included in the canon of Scripture—letting the world know how a useless runaway became useful through the transforming power of the Cross.

Right now, before going any further, stop and spend some time in prayer. Thank God for His great love for you, the love that sent the grace of His own Son to bring you near to Him. Soak in that gift of love and grace.

———◆———

Now, if Paul were to write a letter to you, to whom would he urge you to extend God's grace? To welcome as an equal, a beloved brother or sister, in Christ? Think about this, and in your thinking, go beyond just the slavery scenario in Philemon. Today's parallels would be more along the lines of race, creed, social standing, income level, education.

_____

_____

_____

_____

We all enter God's kingdom by grace. Not by any merit of our own, not by any "specialness" that's better than others. We come by God's love alone. A love that is deep and wide and long and tall enough to encompass everybody. If we've received such a bounty from God's open arms, how can we not open our arms to others?

Chapter 6

HEBREWS: JESUS CHRIST, OUR SUPERIOR SAVIOR

A Survey of Hebrews

Angels.

They are God's messengers. His shining servants. His splendid soldiers. The most magnificent of created beings.

As part of God's revealed truth in the Scriptures, angels deserve our attention and study. Just walk into any bookstore, though, and you'll see that many best-selling authors have departed drastically from Scripture and taken angels to an extreme. Some have even deified angels and assigned them spiritual supremacy. If we're not careful, we can elevate angels to a position of devotion and worship they were never meant to occupy.

There is only one Person worthy of that kind of affection. Only one who holds our lives in His hands. Only one who guides with infallible truth. Only one through whom we can enter the heavenly realm. Jesus Christ Himself.

As the author of Hebrews tells us, Jesus is "much better than the angels, as He has inherited a more excellent name than they" (1:4). He is, in fact, above all things—all man-made religious systems, all people, even the most stalwart of saints, all of creation. He is, as the book of Hebrews tells us, our Superior Savior.

Background of Hebrews

Much about Hebrews remains shrouded in mystery. We're not sure who wrote it or when it was written. Nor can we say with certainty to whom it was written, although its themes and style provide some clues. Nevertheless, considering the background of Hebrews will help set the framework for our study.

Author

Throughout history, various people have been proposed as the author of Hebrews. Clement of Alexandria suggested that Paul wrote it in Hebrew and that Luke translated it into Greek. Jerome and Augustine also popularized the idea of Paul as the author of Hebrews.

HEBREWS

Prologue (1:1–4)
Epilogue (13:20–25)

Jesus Christ: Superior in His Person

Superior to:
- Prophets
- Angels
- Moses
- The Sabbath
- Other priests

CHAPTERS 1:1–4:13

Jesus Christ: Superior as our Priest

Better than:
- Earthly priesthood
- Old covenant (Mosaic system)
- Animal sacrifices
- Daily offerings

CHAPTERS 4:14–10:18

Jesus Christ: Superior for Life

Let us have:
- Faith to believe God
- Hope to endure trials
- Love to encourage others

CHAPTERS 10:19–13:25

Emphasis	Instruction			Exhortation
Key Words	"Much better than . . ." (1:4)	"Better . . ." (7:19)		"Let us . . ." (12:1)
Warnings	(2:1–4) (3:7–4:13)	(5:11–6:20)	(10:19–39)	(12:25–29)
Main Theme	The absolute superiority of Jesus Christ			
Key Verse	"Since we have a great high priest . . . let us hold fast our confession." (4:14)			

If Paul did write Hebrews, though, he departed drastically from his usual manner of writing. The style of Greek is more polished and refined than Paul's normal style. Absent, too, are the apostle's customary greeting and identification of himself as the author. And the phrase "After it was at the first spoken through the Lord, it was confirmed to us by those who heard" (2:3), seems to deny that the writer had firsthand contact with Jesus. Yet in other letters, Paul makes a point of his encountering Jesus personally, thus confirming his apostleship.

Tertullian suggested Barnabas as the author. Others have proposed Clement of Rome, Silas, Philip the Evangelist, the eloquent Apollos of Alexandria, even Priscilla and Aquila. In the end, though, we're compelled to say with Origen, "who wrote the *Letter to the Hebrews* only God knows for certain."[1]

The author's anonymity, however, doesn't hinder Hebrews' inclusion in the canon of Scripture. Its truths about God, humanity, and the atoning work of Christ are consistent with all Scripture. And, though anonymous to us, the writer was apparently known by his readers (13:18–19).

Recipients

To whom was Hebrews written? The Greek title, *Pros Ebraious*, "to the Hebrews," as well as the letter's Old Testament content, tell us the audience was Jewish. The readers had obviously put their faith in Christ (3:1) but were drifting away from the truths they had embraced (2:1). Perhaps they "were on the verge of lapsing into Judaism to avoid persecution directed at Christians."[2] The letter's focus seems to support this idea. Why else would the author so strongly emphasize the superiority of Christianity over Judaism?

Origin and Date

Not knowing the identity of the writer or the recipients makes it impossible to determine the place of writing. A reasonable estimation of the date, however, can be made. Authors Bruce Wilkinson and Kenneth Boa explain that

---

1. William Barclay, *The Letter to the Hebrews*, rev. ed., The Daily Study Bible Series (Philadelphia, Pa.: Westminster Press, 1976), pp. 7–8.

2. Bruce Wilkinson and Kenneth Boa, *Talk Thru the Bible* (Nashville, Tenn.: Thomas Nelson Publishers, 1983), p. 456.

Hebrews was quoted in A.D. 95 by Clement of Rome, but its failure to mention the ending of the Old Testament sacrificial system with the destruction of Jerusalem in A.D. 70 indicates that it was written prior to that date. Timothy was still alive (13:23), persecution was mounting, and the old Jewish system was about to be removed (12:26–27). All this suggests a date between A.D. 64 and 68.[3]

Nero, the sadistic persecutor of Christians, would have been emperor during this time.

Main Theme

Though the author, date, and recipients of Hebrews remain a mystery, there's no mistaking the message.

> The basic theme of Hebrews is found in the use of the word "better" (1:4; 6:9; 7:7, 19, 22; 8:6; 9:23; 10:34; 11:16, 35, 40; 12:24). The words "perfect" and "heavenly" are also prominent in describing the superiority of Christ in His person and work. He offers a better revelation, position, priesthood, covenant, sacrifice, and power. The writer develops this theme to prevent the readers from giving up the substance for the shadow by abandoning Christianity and retreating into the old Judaic system.[4]

Let us look, then, at what this letter tells us about our Superior Savior.

Overall Structure of Hebrews

Following the theme of Christ's superiority, we can organize the letter this way: The superiority of Jesus Christ as a person (1:1–4:13); the superiority of Jesus Christ as our priest (4:14–10:18); the superiority of Jesus Christ for living the Christian life (10:19–13:25).

3. Wilkinson and Boa, *Talk Thru the Bible*, p. 456.

4. Wilkinson and Boa, *Talk Thru the Bible*, p. 456.

Jesus Christ: The Superior Person (1:1–4:13)

Dispensing with any greeting or introduction, the author launches immediately into his topic: the surpassing greatness of Jesus Christ. As God's final and finest revelation, He surpasses the prophets. As the atoning Son and all-powerful King, He is more splendid and majestic than the angels. And as our Savior and Sustainer, His glory outshines that of Moses.

Better Than the Prophets

The author immediately connects Jesus with Judaism and the Old Testament by presenting Him as the ultimate revelation of God. Though God spoke "long ago to the fathers in the prophets in many portions and in many ways, in these last days [He] has spoken to us in His Son" (1:1–2).

The writer obviously wants to assure his readers that the Gospel of Christ isn't adverse to Judaism (as the Judaizers or other "faith plus works" proponents were claiming). Rather, Jesus is the climactic expression of Judaism. The prophets, though speaking God's words, were only forerunners of the Word Himself, who made all things and is heir to all things (v. 2).

No prophet could claim that he created anything or that he owned any of it. Nor could the prophets say they were "the radiance of [God's] glory and the exact representation of His nature" (v. 3). Though they spoke for God, Jesus *was* God in the flesh. And He upholds all things "by the word of His power" (v. 3).

Better Than the Angels

And only Jesus, being God, could die as an atonement for sin, then ascend to the right hand of the throne of God (v. 3). Doing so, he obtained honor and recognition higher than the angels (v. 4).

Quoting several Old Testament passages, the author shows that Jesus, unlike the angels, is God's only begotten Son (v. 5). The angels worship Him and are subordinate to Him (vv. 6–7). He is the eternal, unchanging God who rules over all (vv. 8–13). Angels, in fact, are sent to minister to those redeemed by Christ (v. 14).

Given Christ's supremacy, then, the author urges his readers to "pay closer attention" to the Gospel message they had embraced so they would not drift away from it (2:1). In the Old Testament, the

Law ("the word spoken through angels", v. 2)[5] carried with it penalties for disobedience. How much more a price would one pay for neglecting "so great a salvation" (v. 3), the Gospel of Christ?

All of creation is subject to Christ and will one day be "under His feet" (v. 8). We won't, however, visibly see Jesus' total domination of creation until He returns. For now, we know Him as Savior, who was for a little while made "lower than the angels"—human—in order to suffer and bring us to glory (vv. 9–18).

Better Than Moses

The writer then draws a comparison between Jesus and Moses. Moses was faithful in all God's house (3:2). But Christ, as the builder of His house, exercised the perfect faithfulness of a Son (vv. 3–6a). Commentator Leon Morris sheds light on this comparison:

> Moses was no more than a part of the "house," but Jesus made the house. Again, Jesus as Son was over the house, whereas Moses was a servant in it. The "house," of course, is the household, the people, not the building; and it is God's house, the people of God. Moses was a member of that house and proved faithful there . . . [but] he was essentially one with all the others. Christ has an innate superiority. He is the Son and as such is "over" the household.[6]

That's not to take anything away from Moses' shining example of faithfulness. But Christ is even more faithful. Moses and his ministry, as crucial as they were to the people of God, fade in comparison to the glorious person and work of Christ.

Those of us who embrace Christ by faith are part of His household, the church (v. 6b). And by believing in and walking with Him (vv. 7–19), we enter His rest—eternal life (chap. 4).

Jesus Christ: The Superior Priest (4:14–10:18)

Our rest is predicated upon Christ's work. He is the great High

---

5. Several Scriptures indicate that angels were involved in the giving of the Law at Sinai (Deut. 33:2; Acts 7:53; Gal. 3:19). The Law, of course, didn't originate with angels, but they may have been present to mark the occasion. After all, they were active messengers when the Word became flesh.

6. Leon Morris, "Hebrews," *The Expositor's Bible Commentary*, gen. ed. Frank E. Gaebelein (Grand Rapids, Mich.: Zondervan Publishing House, Regency Reference Library, 1981), vol. 12, pp. 31–32.

Priest who intercedes for us to assuage God's judgment. The author devotes the letter's largest section to the exploration of Jesus' ministry as our great high priest. Unlike earthly priests, whose ministry was temporary, Jesus is our eternal intercessor and advocate before the Father. His covenant is a new and better one. And His sacrifice is pure, perfect, and forever.

Like, Yet Unlike, the Aaronic Priesthood

The priests of old, the descendants of Aaron, passed into the Holy of Holies in the tabernacle to enter the presence of God. But Jesus, our "great high priest" (4:14), "passed through the heavens" at his ascension and stands forever in the presence of God. And, unlike the priests of old, Jesus was "tempted in all things as we are, yet without sin" (v. 15), so He stands ready to help us in temptation.

Christ's ministry is the perfect fulfillment of the Aaronic priesthood. Priests "were identified with the weak and erring people whom they represented (5:1–3) and served at God's appointment"[7] (v. 4). Likewise, Christ served by the Father's appointment (vv. 5–6) and identified with His people through suffering (vv. 7–10). Christ's ministry differed, though, in that He didn't have to offer atonement for His own sin, for He had none.

Press on to Maturity

The readers should know and be teaching these truths by now. But they're still living on "milk" (v. 12) instead of on the nourishing meat of the Word. They need to "press on to maturity" (6:1) and avoid slipping back into a rigid Old Testament understanding of the spiritual life (vv. 1–3). For it is possible for some to have exposure to Christian truth and later fall away (vv. 4–6), demonstrating that their faith was not real. True faith, rooted in the Gospel, yields a life of blessing and good works (vv. 7–8).

Having addressed the possibility of apostasy, the writer assures his "beloved" readers (v. 9) that he is confident they will progress. To endure to the end, though, they must shake off their present sluggishness (v. 11–12). They, like Abraham, can press ahead in the spiritual life, trusting in the sure promises of God and the perfect priestly ministry of Jesus (vv. 13–20), who is our "high priest forever according to the order of Melchizedek" (v. 20).

---

7. *New Geneva Study Bible*, gen. ed. R. C. Sproul, New Testament editor Moisés Silva (Nashville, Tenn.: Thomas Nelson Publishers, 1995), p. 193.

Jesus, A Priest Like Melchizedek

Just who was this Melchizedek, to whom Jesus is compared? His name means "king of righteousness." He was the king of Salem who blessed Abraham and offered him a tithe after the patriarch had won a battle (see Gen. 14:18–20).

Scripture is silent as to Melchizedek's ancestry and progeny (Heb. 7:3). And that is the author's point. This king-priest obtained his position, not by genealogy, but by divine appointment.

The same is true with Jesus. It wasn't earthly credentials that qualified Him as our eternal priest, but His appointment as the perfect divine priest. Jesus descended from the tribe of Judah, not the priestly line of Levi (v. 14). This points to the divine nature of Jesus' priesthood and to the new and better covenant He mediates. Priests who administered sacrifices under the Law eventually died (v. 23). Jesus, however, "abides forever" and holds a permanent priesthood (v. 24). He saves us and keeps us secure by providing unfailing intercession before the Father (v. 25).

He is the perfect priest who offered the perfect sacrifice—Himself. Jesus, the spotless Son of God, did what the Law and the priesthood could not do. He provided a one-time sacrifice sufficient for all people, for all time. So those who are in Christ are part of a new and better covenant than the Law (v. 28).

The Eternal Duties of the Perfect Priest

In chapters 8–10 the author graphically illustrates that the whole Old Testament priestly system was merely a shadow of Christ's role. The priests could enter the Holy of Holies, beyond the "second veil" (9:3), only through the bloody sacrifice of animals. Christ, our heavenly priest and ultimate sacrifice, has allowed us to enter the heavenly Holy of Holies through His one-time atoning death.

The sacrifices of animals, no matter how frequent, couldn't completely purify people (10:1). If the sacrifices could have cleansed completely, they would have needed to be offered only once. Jesus, on the other hand, "has perfected for all time those who are sanctified" (v. 14). His atoning sacrifice does away with the need for sin offerings (v. 18).

Jesus Christ: The Superior Source for Living (10:19–13:25)

With the words "Since therefore" (10:19), the writer now sets forth the applications of the truths he has just explained. Since Jesus has provided access to the God of heaven, the readers can "draw near" (v. 22) to Him, knowing they've been cleansed from sin by the blood of the Lamb.

They can "hold fast" to their beliefs, knowing that Jesus will not fail them (v. 23). And since Christians are a community of interdependent people, they are to "stimulate one another to love and good deeds" and avoid forsaking assembling for worship (vv. 24–25).

Those who reject Christ, though, can expect judgment, just as those under the Law faced judgment for rejecting the Law (vv. 26–31).

In the past, the readers had held fast to their faith during suffering (vv. 32–39), so now they should stand strong and not "shrink back" (v. 39) when faced with the temptation to return to Judaism. After all, they "have faith to the preserving of the soul" (v. 39).

Faith Defined and Depicted

With the temptation to drift back into a works-based righteousness, the readers needed a fresh lesson on what faith was. The author defines it as "the assurance of things hoped for, the conviction of things not seen" (11:1).

To illustrate the results of true faith, the writer points to some Old and New Testament believers, showing how they trusted God to bless, provide, protect, lead, conquer, and give life—even in the most dire circumstances (vv. 4–40). Special emphasis is given to Abraham, the father of the Jewish nation. If his relationship with God was based on faith, how could these first-century Hebrews abandon faith for salvation by works?

Next, the writer directs his readers to fix their eyes on the "author and perfecter of faith" (12:2), Jesus Christ. Having endured the Cross and now seated in heaven, He is both our source of faith and the ultimate example of it (vv. 2–4).

Renewed Spirituality

The recipients of this letter might have been assuming that the suffering and persecution they faced were signs of God's disfavor. The writer, however, exhorts them to view hardship as a sign of God's love. For the Lord disciplines those who belong to Him in order to mature them (vv. 4–11).

The writer also urges them to live real and vital lives. After all, through Christ, they have the power to pursue spiritual healing, peace with all people, and personal holiness (vv. 12–17).

The readers, and we, are able to live the Christian life because the insufficiency and limited access of the old covenant has been replaced with the glorious completeness and openness of the new (vv. 18–24).

The God of the new covenant, however, is still the same God, and He will judge those who reject Him. For "our God is a consuming fire" (v. 29).

Continue in Love

As the writer begins to wrap up his letter, he exhorts his readers to "let love of the brethren continue" (13:1). By being hospitable to strangers, remembering the plight of prisoners, holding marriage in high esteem, and practicing contentment, they will show the love of Christ (vv. 1–6).

Follow Christ

By imitating the faith of those who taught them, the readers will display the unchangeable Christ. It is His grace, through His atoning sacrifice—not our religious practice—that keeps us secure in Him.

Our response to Him should not be offering animal sacrifices, but offering a "sacrifice of praise," that is, giving thanks, doing good, and sharing with others (vv. 15–16).

After urging his readers to submit joyfully to their leaders, and after asking for prayer for his own life and conduct, the author closes with a benediction that summarizes his Christ-exalting letter:

> Now the God of peace, who brought up from the dead the great Shepherd of the sheep through the blood of the eternal covenant, even Jesus our Lord, equip you in every good thing to do His will, working in us that which is pleasing in His sight, through Jesus Christ, to whom be the glory forever and ever. Amen. . . . Grace be with you all. (vv. 20–25)

Superior grace . . . from a superior Savior. That's what we have. And that's even better than being touched by an angel.

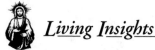 *Living Insights*

"Son, if I didn't love you, I'd just let you go your own way. I wouldn't care whether or not you learned how to make responsible choices. My discipline is a sure sign that I love you."

Loving parents want their kids to understand that discipline and love aren't mutually exclusive ideas—that spankings and other forms of correction are not vents for parental anger, outbursts of frustration, or clubs wielded to abuse authority (and children). Instead, parents want their kids to understand that real love *requires* discipline.

So why do we have such a hard time receiving discipline from our heavenly Father? I don't know about you, but I must admit that my goal in life is, too often, comfort. Freedom from pain. Financial security. Approval and encouragement from all who know me. A computer that works like it's supposed to. You know, heaven on earth.

How different from God's perspective. His goal is to conform us to His image, to make us holy (Heb. 12:4–11). In fact, He assures us that never experiencing His discipline is reason to wonder if we really belong to Him (v. 8).

Do you need some encouragement that God loves you? Don't just look at the comforts He provides. Consider the discomfort He brings into your life as well. They are tools of correction in the hands of your loving Father.

Sure, it hurts. But metal bends better when softened with fire. Marble takes shape only under the splintering blow of a chisel. And whoever heard of smoothing wood without the abrasive scrape of sandpaper?

A loving God using pain to produce good in His children may sound harsh, until you consider that the most loving thing He ever did was also the most painful—putting His only Son on the Cross.

Let us welcome and endure His discipline, for it "yields the peaceful fruit of righteousness" (v. 11).

Chapter 7

JAMES: A PLEA
FOR AUTHENTICITY

A Survey of James

D~oes it work?"

That's a question we all ask when we're about to buy something. Sure, that stereo boasts plenty of nice features—programmable play, remote control, etc.—but how does it perform? Does the CD changer operate smoothly and quietly? Does the radio pick up signals loud and clear? And what about those speakers? Do they separate all the fine audio nuances and pump out the decibels? After all, who would lay down hard-earned cash for a stereo system that only sounds good in theory?

Likewise, who would buy into a belief system that fails to produce real change in a person's life? According to James, that kind of Christianity isn't Christianity at all. Genuine faith produces good works in the life of a believer.

Are you looking for some encouragement that the faith you've sold out to really does work? That because you have put your faith in Christ, you can really change? That your faith can endure, even increase, in times of hardship? Good. Then let's open the epistle of James together—and learn anew that Jesus died and rose again, not just to deliver us from God's wrath, but to develop us into His likeness.

Background of James

Though James' letter is among the most practical and straightforward sections of Scripture, understanding the epistle's background will provide even more insight into the author's words.

Author

Four men in the New Testament bear the name of James: (1) the brother of John, one of the sons of Zebedee (Mark 1:19), (2) the son of Alphaeus (Mark 3:18), (3) the father of Judas (not Iscariot; Luke 6:16), and (4) the half brother of Jesus (Gal. 1:19).

The son of Alphaeus, though listed as a disciple, is relatively

58

JAMES

Faith . . .	When stretched it doesn't break	When pressed it doesn't fail	When expressed it doesn't explode	When distressed it doesn't panic
Deeds	Authentic stability	Authentic love	Authentic control and humility	Authentic patience
	Greeting	Partiality and prejudice	The tongue	Money matters
	Trials	Indifference and mere intellectualism	The heart	Sickness
	Temptation	Obedience and action	The will	Carnality and correction
	Response to Scripture			
	CHAPTER 1	CHAPTER 2	CHAPTERS 3–4	CHAPTER 5

Background	The difficulties of life caused the scattered saints to drift spiritually, leading to all forms of problems—unbridled speech, wrong attitudes, doubt, strife, carnality, shallow faith.
Characteristics	"The Proverbs of the New Testament," James contains many practical, straightforward exhortations. Emphasis is on importance of balancing right belief with right behavior. Many Old Testament word pictures and references.
Main Theme	Real faith produces authentic deeds.
Key Verse	"Even so faith, if it has no works, is dead, being by itself." (2:17)

59

obscure, as is James the father of Judas. The letter could have been written by James the brother of John, although he was martyred in 44 B.C. This would place the letter's writing at a date most scholars believe is too early to consider reasonable. So the best candidate for the writing of this epistle is James the Lord's half brother. Authors Bruce Wilkinson and Kenneth Boa provide a literary rationale for this view:

> There are several clear parallels between the language of the letter drafted under [James'] leadership in Acts 15:23–29 and the epistle of James. . . . The Jewish character of this epistle with its stress upon the Law, along with the evident influence by the Sermon on the Mount (e.g., 4:11–12; 5:12), complement what we know about James "the Just" from Scripture and early tradition.[1]

Commentator Donald W. Burdick adds that the "authoritative tone of the epistle . . . agrees well with the authority exercised by James in Acts 15:13ff.; 21:18."[2]

Though apparently none of Jesus' siblings believed in Him during His earthly ministry (John 7:5), James did eventually come to faith in Him, perhaps after seeing the risen Lord (1 Cor. 15:7). James went on to become one of the "pillars of the church" (Gal. 2:9).

Date

Assuming, then, that James the Lord's half brother is the author, when did he write the epistle? It's difficult to pinpoint the exact date, but we can get close.

Historian Flavius Josephus places James' martyrdom around A.D. 62. And there are many good reasons to believe the letter was written even before A.D. 49.

First, James doesn't mention the Jerusalem council of A.D. 49, an event in which he played a significant role and which crystallized the church's official attitude toward Gentile believers (see Acts 15).

Second, the Jewish flavor of the epistle and the absence of any

---

1. Bruce Wilkinson and Kenneth Boa, *Talk Thru the Bible* (Nashville, Tenn.: Thomas Nelson Publishers, 1983), pp. 463–64.

2. Donald W. Burdick, "James," in *The Expositor's Bible Commentary*, gen. ed. Frank E. Gaebelein (Grand Rapids, Mich.: Zondervan Publishing House, Regency Reference Library, 1981), vol. 12, p. 161.

language emphasizing the melding of Jews and Gentiles into one body suggests an early date, when the church was still predominately Jewish. For example, the letter's recipients, the "twelve tribes" (James 1:1), suggests a Jewish readership. The word "assembly" (2:2) is the same word used for "synagogue," the primary meeting place for the early church. And there is no mention of Jew/Gentile friction, which developed as the church grew.

Third, the letter suggests simple church order (just teachers and elders), rather than the more developed organization and offices found in later writings, such as the pastoral epistles.

Most scholars believe that James wrote his letter some time between A.D. 45 and 49, which would make it the oldest book in the New Testament. Yet, for all its age, this letter is as applicable to us as it was to its original readers.

Style

The book of James "is as much a lecture as it is a letter,"[3] apparently prepared for public reading. Its sentences are short, simple, and to the point; its language is vivid and concrete. Though intended to promote action more than propound theology, the letter exhibits an unmistakable kinship with other books of the Bible. Its pithy nuggets of practical truth resemble the Proverbs. Its "dos" and "do nots" emit echoes of the Mosaic Law and Jesus' Sermon on the Mount. James refers to Abraham, Rahab, Job, and Elijah and alludes to twenty-one Old Testament books.

Theological Considerations

Because of its urgent and imperative tone (fifty-four commands in just 108 verses), James has been maligned by some who have thought it too law-oriented and contrary to the gospel of grace. Even Martin Luther, who at first considered the book insubstantial, once called it "a right strawy epistle."[4] Later, though, he considered it a genuine part of the canon.

While the task of James is not to expound the doctrine of justification by faith, as Paul did in so many of his letters, James'

---

3. J. Ronald Blue, "James," in *The Bible Knowledge Commentary*, New Testament edition, ed. John F. Walvoord and Roy B. Zuck (Wheaton, Ill.: Scripture Press Publications, Victor Books, 1983), p. 816.

4. Wilkinson and Boa, *Talk Thru the Bible*, p. 466.

words are not adverse to the Gospel. Rather, they portray the natural outgrowth of a life saved by grace. As commentator J. Ronald Blue explains,

> Together Paul and James give the full dimension of faith. Paul wrote about inner saving faith from God's perspective. James wrote about outward serving faith from man's perspective. The true seed of saving faith is verified by the tangible fruit of serving faith. James' point is that biblical faith works.[5]

James, then, does not contradict Paul, but complements him, showing how faith in Christ changes lives.

Structure of James

James' letter can be organized around faith's response to life. When faith is stretched, it doesn't break (chap. 1). It retains its strength during trials and temptations and holds fast to the Word. When faith is pressed, it doesn't fail (chap. 2). It dispenses with partiality and extends love to all. In fact, genuine faith shows itself in a variety of good works. When faith is expressed, it doesn't explode (chaps. 3–4). A life of faith is a controlled life, keeping the tongue and emotions in check—and wisdom in the driver's seat. When faith is distressed, it doesn't panic (chap. 5). It trusts God for material possessions, health, and moral purity.

Let's take a closer look, now, at this book of faith—so that our faith may grow.

Faith: Standing Strong in Trials and Temptations (Chap. 1)

After a short salutation, James moves right into the topic most pressing to his readers—trials and temptations.

From James to the Twelve Tribes

James identifies himself as a "bond-servant of God and of the Lord Jesus Christ" (1:1a). James grew up as Jesus' younger half brother, a member of the Lord's earthly family. At some point, though, James became part of Jesus' spiritual family. He recognized Jesus for who He was, and Jesus became more than James' sibling; He became his Savior.

5. Blue, "James," p. 816.

The recipients, "the twelve tribes who are dispersed abroad" (1:1b), were probably Jewish Christians who had been persecuted and driven out of Jerusalem by anti-Christian Jews. They were now scattered among the nations.

Knowing many of them had suffered personal and financial loss, James sought to encourage them.

The Purpose of Trials

"Consider it all joy," says James, "when you encounter various trials" (v. 2). This is more than shallow advice to "grin and bear it" or a lesson on positive thinking. There really is a reason to rejoice when hardship comes our way. Trials test our faith—not so God can see whether we will pass or fail, but so He can reconfirm to us that He is sufficient and trustworthy.

Trials produce endurance (v. 3). How else would we learn to persevere and trust Him if we never had to struggle? But endurance isn't an end in itself. It renders us "perfect and complete, lacking in nothing" (v. 4). This isn't a promise of sinless perfection—for that, we have to wait for heaven. But it is a promise that we will develop into mature Christians if we persevere under pressure.

Wisdom for the Asking

That's not to say, however, that persevering through trials is easy, or that it comes naturally. For those perplexed about how to persevere, James urges them to ask for wisdom and reassures them that it will be given by our gracious God (vv. 5–8).

Trials know no social class. Whether rich or poor, believers must look beyond earthly life to the eternal God, who sustains us during hardship (vv. 9–11).

A Blessing for the Persevering

Those who persevere under trials are blessed, for they will receive the "crown of life" (v. 12). This crown is, ultimately, eternal life, but it may also refer to a more blessed quality of life on earth as a result of trusting God.

Trials brought by God for our testing, however, are not to be confused with temptation that grows out of our own sinful desires (vv. 13–15). These lead to sinful actions and eventually to death. No, God is not an enticer. He who never wavers in His goodness is the Giver of all good gifts, including new life in Christ (vv. 16–18).

A Right Response to the Word

Ultimately, enduring trials and temptations comes down to being "doers" of the Word (v. 22). With a listening ear and an absence of anger and pride, we must listen to what God has said, internalize it, and act on it (vv. 19–21; 23–25). Only then can we demonstrate such true religion as bridling our tongue and helping the needy (vv. 26–27).

Faith: Succeeding in Serving Others (Chap. 2)

In chapter 2 James continues to show us what true religion and real faith look like.

Love Your Neighbor

God's Word commands us to love our neighbor as ourselves (2:8). That includes avoiding prejudice or partiality (vv. 1–7). If we show preference to the rich and ignore the poor, we're transgressing God's Law (vv. 8–13).

Faith and Works

Having given several illustrations of faith, James now gives us the theme of the whole book: real faith produces authentic deeds. Saving faith is demonstrative faith (v. 14). It goes beyond words and reaches out to the needy (vv. 15–16). Faith that fails to produce good deeds is dead and useless (vv. 17, 20, 26). And merely declaring a belief in one God is not necessarily a sign of true faith either. Even demons do that (v. 19).

Abraham, though saved long before God asked him to offer up Isaac, demonstrated faith by obeying God (vv. 21–23). Rahab, the prostitute in Jericho, demonstrated her faith by lending aid to the Israelite army (v. 25). Works, while not producing salvation, are the demonstration of true saving faith (v. 24).[6]

---

6. Verse 24 says we're "justified by works and not by faith alone." This seems to contradict Paul's statement that "a man is justified by faith apart from works of the Law" (Rom. 3:28). But it doesn't. Paul was explaining how one *gains entrance* into salvation. James is examining how one *gives evidence* of it. God justifies us (declares us righteous) by giving us the gift of eternal life. That comes by faith in Christ alone; we can't earn it. But, after we're saved, we're also "justified" (shown to be saved) by the deeds we do. Thus, there are two senses of the word "justify." We're not saved because we do good deeds—we do good deeds because we're saved.

Faith: Expressed through Self-Control (Chaps. 3–4)

James transitions once again to more specific manifestations of faith, beginning with controlled speech.

Taming the Tongue

Moving into the topic of the tongue, James warns his readers not to be too eager to teach the Scriptures. Since teachers use their tongues often, they have more opportunities to misrepresent the Scriptures and thus "incur a stricter judgment" (3:1).

The truth is that we all have a hard time controlling our tongues (vv. 2–10). But, just as a fountain sends out only one kind of water and a tree produces only one kind of fruit, the speech of the believer should be consistent with his or her new life in Christ (vv. 11–12).

Faith also produces a life of godly wisdom, not earthly ambition (vv. 13–18).

Keeping Desires in Check

James' readers also needed help controlling their desires. Their selfish pursuit of personal pleasure was causing division among them (4:1). Instead of asking God for what they needed, they were coveting, even murdering (vv. 2–3). They had fallen in love with the world (vv. 4–6).

But James offers them a way out: "Submit therefore to God. Resist the devil and he will flee from you" (v. 7). By humbling ourselves before God and seeking His help, we can sidestep the world's snares (vv. 8–10). Humility also enables us to avoid slandering and judging others (vv. 11–12).

Arrogance and pride have no place in the Christian life. Our lives are completely in God's hands; we could be gone tomorrow in a wisp of smoke. Therefore, we must live trusting Him for every moment (vv. 13–17).

Faith: Steady When Distressed (Chap. 5)

Some of James' wealthy readers, though, were looking at life as an opportunity to hoard material wealth. They were taking advantage of others, even killing them, in order to fill their coffers.

Warnings to the Rich, Encouragement for the Poor

James warns these abusive materialists that their possessions are only temporal and that they will have to face the Lord for what they have done (5:1–6). On the other hand, he encourages the poor who have been abused by the rich to be patient and avoid turning on one another, for the Lord will return (vv. 7–9). Their suffering will one day disappear, just like the treasures of the rich. As with the prophets and Job, the perseverance of the poor will be met with the Lord's compassion and mercy (vv. 10–11).

One way to demonstrate trust and patience in the Lord is to avoid careless and flippant oaths and, instead, let one's word stand on its own (v. 12).

Final Exhortations

James brings his letter to a close with a final list of exhortations about how to respond to various circumstances. He exhorts the suffering to pray, the cheerful to sing, and the sick to call on the elders for prayer (vv. 13–15).

Emphasizing the importance of community, he urges them to confess their sins to and pray for one another. For "the effective prayer of a righteous man can accomplish much" (vv. 16–18).

It's doubtful that anyone reading James' words would have considered himself able to do everything the author asked. Therefore, it would have been encouraging to know that those who stray from the truth could be brought back "from the error of [their] way" (vv. 19–20).

We need to remember that. None of us consistently produces actions that verify our faith in Christ. We drift in and out of godly living. Yet our hope is not in how well we live but in how well Christ lived—and died—on our behalf (2 Cor. 5:21). Our salvation is secure in Him and in Him alone (John 10:27–29).

When we blow it, we can rest in Jesus Christ's perfect work on the Cross. Because we belong to Him, He always stands ready to welcome straying sheep back into His fold through repentance and restoration (1 John 1:9).

Does Christianity work? You bet it does. And it's guaranteed to last a lifetime—an eternal lifetime.

 Living Insights

It seems that we rarely realize the benefit of trials when we're in the midst of them. That usually comes with hindsight. Have you found that to be true? Thinking back over the past year or two, list a couple of trials that tested your faith.

_____

_____

_____

_____

_____

_____

_____

Can you think of any good that came out of them? Did you learn something new about God? About yourself? About those around you?

_____

_____

_____

_____

_____

_____

Now, how do those memories—and the words of James in 1:2–18 —give you hope for the difficulties you're facing right now?

_____

_____

_____

_____

_____

_____

Chapter 8

1 PETER: HOPE
FOR THE HURTING

A Survey of 1 Peter

What a picture of the Christian life the apostle Peter is. In his journey of faith, we don't find a smooth, steady ascent up the heights of ever-increasing glory. We find, instead, reality, with all its winding, dipping, stumbling, steadying, discouraging, and breathtaking twists and turns. His path is our path—the walk of faith not always as we think it should be, but often as it is.

Nowhere do we see this more clearly than when it comes to accepting suffering.

When Jesus asked His disciples who they thought He was, Peter joyfully proclaimed, "You are the Christ, the Son of the living God" (Matt. 16:16). But when Jesus presented His plan of suffering, Peter was aghast. He even took it upon himself to rebuke the Son of the living God: "God forbid it, Lord!" (v. 22).

And don't we do the same thing? Don't we want triumph instead of trials? Power instead of pain? Escape instead of endurance? Don't we try to tell God how things ought to be done? And scold Him when He does things differently?

We want the glory of the Second Coming—and rightly so. However, the only way to get to the Second Coming is to live in Jesus' present coming, which is the way of the Cross.

Peter eventually came to understand this; and in his first letter, he shared the wisdom God gave him concerning our present journey. He matured into a most worthy guide, and we would do well to follow his lead along the rocky path called the Christian life.

The Background of 1 Peter

First Peter has been called "a handbook written for ambassadors to a hostile foreign land."[1] Let's see what was going on at the time to merit this description.

---

1. Roger M. Raymer, "1 Peter," in *The Bible Knowledge Commentary*, New Testament edition, ed. John F. Walvoord and Roy B. Zuck (Wheaton, Ill.: Scripture Press Publications, Victor Books, 1983), p. 838.

1 PETER

Salutation (1:1–2) — Conclusion (5:12–14)

	Our Living Hope and Holy Life	Our Submission and God's Honor	Our Suffering and Christ's Suffering
	"Blessed be the God and Father of our Lord Jesus Christ ..." (1:3)	"Submit yourselves for the Lord's sake ..." (2:13)	"Since Christ has suffered ..." (4:1)
	... for the hope we claim (1:3–12)	... to the government (2:13–17)	Keep a good conscience (3:16)
	... by our walk of holiness (1:13–25)	... at work (2:18–20)	Share the sufferings and rejoice (4:13)
	... for our new identity in Christ (2:1–12)	... like Christ (2:21–25)	Commit yourselves to God (4:19)
		... in the home (3:1–7)	Be humble (5:6)
			Cast your anxiety on God (5:7)
	CHAPTERS 1:3–2:12	*CHAPTERS 2:13–3:7*	*CHAPTERS 3:8–5:11*
Emphasis	Informing	Exhorting	Encouraging
Grace	... to go on	... to live faithfully	... to stand firm
Hope	A *living* hope through Christ's resurrection (1:3)	A *righteous* hope through personal submission (2:15)	A *trusting* hope through faith (4:19)
Main Themes	Holy living in a hostile world; hope in the midst of suffering		
Key Verses	1:3–5, 13–16; 2:21; 4:12–13, 19; 5:10–11		

Author and Date

The apostle Peter wrote this letter around A.D. 63, before Nero's terrible persecution—in which Peter was eventually martyred. The early church fathers explicitly supported Peter's authorship; however, modern critics have debated whether Peter was actually the author. They believe that the polished quality of the original Greek would have been too fine for Peter, a rough-spoken Galilean. They also date the epistle later to reflect the government-sponsored persecution of Christians under the emperors Domitian (A.D. 81–96) and Trajan (A.D. 98–117).

The first argument can be answered from a clue in the letter itself: in 5:12, Peter credits Silvanus (also known as Silas) with helping him write the letter—probably writing Peter's thoughts down in good literary Greek. The second objection assumes that Christians didn't experience persecution earlier in the century, which we know from the book of Acts is false. Persecution may not have been an official government policy, but it was real nevertheless.

Recipients

According to 1:1, Peter wrote to "those who reside as aliens, scattered throughout Pontus, Galatia, Cappadocia, Asia, and Bithynia"—regions that comprise most of modern-day Turkey. These communities probably had some Jewish believers, since Jews from Cappadocia, Pontus, and Asia were converted through Peter's sermon at Pentecost (see Acts 2:9). But judging from many of Peter's phrases in the letter—for example, "your futile way of life inherited from your forefathers" (1 Pet. 1:18), "for you once were not a people" (2:10), "they are surprised that you do not run with them into the same excesses of dissipation, and they malign you" (4:4)— his recipients were predominantly Gentile.

Themes

More important, though, than geography and ethnicity are Peter's descriptions of his readers as "aliens" and "scattered." For in these words we find one of Peter's major themes: that Christians are "resident aliens" in this world and citizens of another, better world—a world opened to us at a precious cost, with a life to be lived at the most high and holy standards.

The powers of this present world, however, are hostile toward God's kingdom; so they attack, and we suffer, just as Christ suffered (see John 15:18–20). Jesus' suffering and our sharing in it is another of Peter's major themes, as commentator Edwin A. Blum explains.

> Not only is [Jesus'] death a substitutionary atonement (2:24), but at the same time it provides a pattern for Christian living. Since Jesus was the Suffering Servant, his followers also have a vocation of suffering (2:21).[2]

Peter does not make suffering an end in itself, however. It is purposeful, replete with meaning, and has a definite end in sight: glory. For just as Christ first suffered and was then glorified, so we follow Him from suffering into glory. This is our hope; and hope in the midst of suffering is a prominent theme throughout Peter's letter.

Style and Structure

Peter's tone is warm and encouraging; he speaks as a gentle, experienced pastor who has faithfully kept Jesus' charge to "Shepherd My sheep" (John 21:15–17). He begins his letter with a salutation that establishes a rich theological foundation for all that will follow (1 Pet. 1:1–2). Then he describes our living hope and holy life (1:3–2:12), explains our submissive, Christlike lifestyle (2:13–3:7), and counsels us regarding our suffering for Christ (3:8–5:11). Finally, he concludes with encouragement, greetings, and peace (5:12–5:14).

Salutation (1:1–2)

> Peter, an apostle of Jesus Christ,
>
> To those who reside as aliens, scattered throughout Pontus, Galatia, Cappadocia, Asia, and Bithynia, who are chosen according to the foreknowledge of God the Father, by the sanctifying work of the Spirit, to obey Jesus Christ and be sprinkled with His blood: May grace and peace be yours in the fullest measure. (1:1–2)

---

2. Edwin A. Blum, "1 Peter," in *The Expositor's Bible Commentary*, gen. ed. Frank E. Gaebelein (Grand Rapids, Mich.: Zondervan Publishing House, Regency Reference Library, 1981), vol. 12, p. 215.

Right from the start, Peter establishes his readers' new identity, which is grounded in the work of the entire Trinity. Clearly, the remarkable thing about our salvation is not that we have chosen God—but that He has chosen us! As the Father foreknew Christ "before the foundation of the world" (v. 20), so He has foreknown and elected us for salvation. His Spirit has set apart the Father's chosen ones for His appointed service (see Eph. 2:10), leading us to obey Christ and be continually cleansed of our sins by His blood.

With each member of the Trinity working on our behalf, how could grace and peace not be ours in abundance!

Our Living Hope and Holy Life (1:3–2:12)

At the thought of God's wonderful gift of salvation, Peter can only praise Him.

> Blessed be the God and Father of our Lord Jesus Christ, who according to His great mercy has caused us to be born again to a living hope through the re-surrection of Jesus Christ from the dead. (1 Pet. 1:3)

For now, we walk in the way of the Cross; but because the Cross was not the end of Christ's story, so it is not our end either. He conquered death and rose to new life, enabling us to be born into His same new life—a life everlasting in the loving presence of God. This is our imperishable inheritance, our ever-living hope. It is kept safe for us in heaven, and we are kept safe for it by God's power (vv. 4–5).

This sure hope brings us a joy that sustains us in the midst of suffering. It helps us realize the true value of our faith, refocusing our eyes and our hearts beyond our temporal trials to eternity with Christ. What joy will be ours when we come into the fullness of our salvation, which we have only clung to by faith during our lives on earth (vv. 6–9)!

For long centuries, the Old Testament prophets foretold this grace and diligently sought to discover the time of its arrival. The very Spirit of Christ was within them, revealing that the Messiah would suffer first but then come into certain glory. This is our pattern too—suffering first, then glory. The Spirit has been fore-telling this gospel throughout time, past and present. And it is so wonderful that even the "angels long to look" into it (vv. 10–12).

In light of such a salvation, Peter tells us to "fix your hope completely on the grace to be brought to you at the revelation of Jesus Christ" (v. 13). We are to be formed, not by our former sins, but by our new life in Christ.

> Like the Holy One who called you, be holy your-
> selves also in all your behavior; because it is written,
> "You shall be holy, for I am holy." (vv. 15–16)

Because we have been redeemed with something precious, the very blood of Christ, we need to live with that reality always before us and honor the One who paid such a price (vv. 17–21). That price was paid not just for each of us individually but for all of us as a community. We're not in the Christian life alone; we have been born into God's everlasting family through His enduring word. And as children of a holy and loving Father, we are to "fervently love one another from the heart," shun every form of hurtful behavior, and seek the spiritual nourishment that will help us mature into the people God has called us to be (1:22–2:3).

Peter changes images in this next, strikingly beautiful section (2:4–12). He sees Christ as the precious cornerstone, rejected by people but chosen by God, upon which His people, as living stones, "are being built up as a spiritual house." As members of His house, we are called to be "a holy priesthood"—we must reflect God's holiness, intercede through prayer for others, and represent God to the world. Many will reject Christ, the precious living stone, and will stumble over Him as "a rock of offense." Because they reject the Life, they will get what they have chosen—eternal death. Those who build on Christ, however, have a different destiny and purpose:

> But you are a chosen race, a royal priesthood, a
> holy nation, a people for God's own possession, so
> that you may proclaim the excellencies of Him who
> has called you out of darkness into His marvelous
> light; for you once were not a people, but now you
> are the people of God; you had not received mercy,
> but now you have received mercy. (vv. 9–10)

Now we must live like the people we are—though we're regarded as nothing by the world—testifying to the reality of God through good works so that others will come to know and glorify Him (vv. 11–12).

Our Submission and God's Honor (2:13–3:7)

"Submit yourselves for the Lord's sake," Peter begins this next section. Doing what is right (notice this idea in 2:15, 20; 3:6) for the Lord's sake no matter the circumstances is essentially what he is getting at.

First, Peter exhorts us to submit to our government leaders. We're not to flaunt our God-given freedom and live by our own rules but serve the good of others and thus serve God (vv. 13–17). Next, Peter urges servants to submit to their masters—even the unreasonable ones. Rather than retaliating, we must again "do what is right," maintaining integrity so that God's new way of living shines forth clearly (vv. 18–20).

All of this, along with what follows in 3:1–6, is grounded in Christ's example of trusting God in the midst of suffering for righteousness' sake. As Jesus, the omnipotent Lord, willingly submitted to His own creatures' authority in order to save us, so we must follow His pattern of humble endurance so that others will be led to His light (vv. 21–25). How could Peter not have been thinking of Jesus' own words to him and his fellow disciples so many years before? "For even the Son of Man did not come to be served, but to serve, and to give His life a ransom for many" (Mark 10:45).

Peter then counsels wives to submit to the authority of their husbands so that, if the husbands are unbelievers, they will be won over to Christ through their wives' respectful behavior (1 Pet. 3:1–2). In other words, our being rescued from sin and having a new, holy way of life should not engender a holier-than-thou, contemptful attitude. In addition, Peter stresses that a woman's true beauty lies not in her external appearance but in "the hidden person of the heart, with the imperishable quality of a gentle and quiet spirit, which is precious in the sight of God" (vv. 3–4). Cultivating this kind of character testifies to the reality of our hope (v. 5).

Peter's example of Sarah (v. 6) is the hinge that takes us from wives respecting their husbands to husbands caring for their wives (v. 7). Sarah called Abraham "lord," a term of respect—not of subservience—for she was also a "fellow heir" of the promises God made to Abraham. Wives today, too, are also "fellow heirs of the grace of life," spiritually equal to their husbands though physically weaker. Husbands, then, must be considerate and kind to their wives. If they run roughshod over them, they damage their relationship with God—their prayers will not be answered.

Our Suffering and Christ's Suffering (3:8–5:11)

"To sum up," Peter writes of the previous section, "all of you be harmonious, sympathetic, brotherly, kindhearted, and humble in spirit" (v. 8). Then, with his next phrase, "not returning evil for evil or insult for insult, but giving a blessing instead," he gently leads us into a more difficult topic: following Christ in the path of suffering.

Through God's grace, we who put our faith in Christ will inherit the blessing of eternal life (v. 9). Peter found an excellent explanation of how we live out this blessing in Psalm 34, which he quotes in verses 10–12. Then, reminding us of Jesus' Beatitude, Peter tells us of another way we are blessed—when we "suffer for the sake of righteousness" (v. 14a; see also Matt. 5:10). Rather than giving in to fear when we are persecuted, we must keep sight of Christ, our Lord, be ready to explain our hope, and also keeping a clear conscience to thwart our enemies' slander (1 Pet. 3:14b–16).

In the next verses, Peter again takes us to his beloved Lord, the just One, who suffered unjustly in order to provide redemption and rescue (vv. 17–20). As He is pure, so we must be pure, abstaining from sin and loving and serving our fellow Christians so that we glorify God (3:21–4:11). We must make sure that we don't suffer through our own fault; suffering for our sins doesn't bring any glory to God. But when we go through the "fiery ordeal" of suffering for following God's will, we can not only endure but rejoice and gain new perspective to continue doing what is right (4:12–19).

In light of the difficulties of suffering faithfully for Christ, Peter turns to those who lead God's flock. And he turns their eyes away from self-interest to the model of the Great Shepherd Himself, Jesus, who will indeed reward their diligent care of His people with the "unfading crown of glory" (5:1–4).

As he wraps up his thoughts, Peter emphasizes the importance of humility with one another, trust in the God who cares so much for us, a keen awareness of our adversary, the need to stand firm in the faith, and the reassurance that glory will certainly follow and dwarf whatever suffering we've been subjected to (vv. 5–10). "To Him be dominion forever and ever. Amen," Peter proclaims (v. 11)!

Conclusion (5:12–14)

After acknowledging Silvanus' help in writing this letter, Peter sums up what he has hoped to accomplish: "exhorting and testifying that this is the true grace of God. Stand firm in it!" (v. 12). He wants us grounded in God's grace. Then he sends greetings from fellow Christians in "Babylon," most likely a code name for Rome, and from his "son," Mark. "Greet one another with a kiss of love," he adds (v. 14a). And in a final benediction, he bestows peace, both to his original readers and to us now.

> Peace be to you all who are in Christ. (v. 14b)

Can you hear the echo of Jesus' words to Peter and the others that last night in the Upper Room?

> "These things I have spoken to you, so that in Me you may have peace. In the world you have tribulation, but take courage; I have overcome the world." (John 16:33)

Take courage, fellow sufferer. For our Master has overcome the world so that our end would not be everlasting pain but eternal life and glory.

 Living Insights

What a rich, rich letter! Take some time to read through it one or two more times, preferably in one sitting, adorning your mind and heart with its myriad of jewels.

To what particular jewel in this letter is the Holy Spirit leading you? To a greater grasp of your living hope? Of the entire Trinity's involvement in your salvation? Is it the worth of your faith? Or your calling to holiness? Is He trying to bring you to a new understanding of the freedom and purpose of submission? Of the redemptive aim of suffering for Christ's sake, in Christ's steps? Is He wanting to lift your weary head to see that suffering is not the end, much like labor is not the end in childbirth, but that glory is?

Use this time to read and to pray and to reflect. Journal, if you like, and don't forget to write down your plan for how you'll apply what the Spirit has put on your heart through Peter's words.

_____

_____

_____

Chapter 9

2 PETER: BEWARE...
BE READY!

A Survey of 2 Peter

If there's one thing we must do, it's to stop underestimating Peter.

All too often, we regard him as a brash, impulsive, bumpkin sort of guy. The cocksure fisherman "indulging" Jesus' desire to let the nets down again, only to nearly capsize with the vast catch of fish (Luke 5:4–7). The daring disciple who wanted to walk on water but sank in doubt (Matt. 14:28–31). The knee-jerk reactor who wouldn't allow Jesus to wash his feet and then impetuously over-corrected himself (John 13:6–9). The overconfident man who said he'd die for Jesus but deserted Him when He needed him most (Mark 14:27–31, 66–72). The intimidated apostle who needed Paul's correction (Gal. 2:11–14).

Rash, blunt, bumbling; a simpleminded, rough-and-tumble fisherman—this is how Peter, unfortunately, gets characterized. But there's another side to Peter. His mistakes are not the whole of him.

Remember, Jesus chose him.

When He raised Jairus's daughter from the dead, Jesus took only Peter, James, and John with Him (Mark 5:35–37). "You are Peter [meaning 'rock'], and upon this rock I will build My church," Jesus said to him (Matt. 16:18). He trusted Peter and John with preparing the Passover for His Last Supper (Luke 22:7–8). Jesus wanted Peter, James, and John to stay closest to Him in the Garden of Gethsemane (Matt. 26:36–38). Jesus had His angel single Peter out by name to come to Him after His resurrection (Mark 16:7). And He took special pains to restore His disciple after his desertion, allowing Peter to reaffirm his love and entrusting His flock to him (John 21:15–17).

It was Peter who recognized that Jesus had the words of eternal life; that He was the Christ, the Holy One of God (John 6:68; Matt. 16:16). It was Peter who gave the first great sermon after Jesus' Ascension on the day of Pentecost, who baptized the first Gentile believer (Acts 2:14–40; 10:34–48). And it was Peter who gave up everything to follow Jesus, both during the Lord's life on earth and forever after (Mark 10:28).

2 PETER

	Introduction (1:1–2)	Exhortation to Spiritual Maturity	Denunciation of False Teachers	Anticipation of Christ's Return
		Answers question: How can I grow in grace and knowledge? (1:2–3)	**Answers question:** What should I expect from so-called prophets?	**Answers question:** What sort of people ought we to be? (3:11)
		CHAPTER 1	*CHAPTER 2*	*CHAPTER 3*
Warning		Be pure! (1:4)	Be aware! (2:1–3)	Be diligent! (3:14)
Reminder		*Verses 12–13*	*Verses 21–22*	*Verses 1–2*
Promise		*"You will never stumble" (v. 10)*	*"The Lord knows how to rescue" (v. 9)*	*"We are looking for new heavens and a new earth" (v. 13)*
Perspective		Looking within	Looking back	Looking ahead
Main Theme		Spiritual maturity as a remedy for false teaching and a right response in light of Christ's second coming		
Key Verses		3:17–18		

79

Would a bumpkin have written such a theologically rich, warm, beautiful, and profound letter as 1 Peter? No. But an earnest, teachable, maturing person could have—one who constantly strove to "grow in the grace and knowledge of our Lord and Savior Jesus Christ" (2 Pet. 3:18). Which is what he would have us do as well, so that rather than our weaknesses defining us, our love of Christ would.

The Background of 2 Peter

Peter's second letter has been the cause of much debate down through the centuries of church history. Let's address and settle some of the issues so that we can proceed with confidence into his message.

Debate over Authorship

Many liberal scholars doubt that the apostle Peter wrote 2 Peter. Their reasons range from the style being too different from that of 1 Peter, to the letter being known only in a limited area, to the doubts spurred by the delay of Christ's return being an issue of a later century.

The answers to these contentions, however, make a much stronger case for Peter's genuine authorship.

First, though the two letters have differences in style, they also address different situations and therefore have different purposes. Also, as we learned in 1 Peter 5:12, Peter had Silvanus's help in writing 1 Peter. Since the apostle does not mention anyone serving in that role in 2 Peter, it's probably safe to assume that Peter either wrote the letter himself or used another amanuensis. Peter, being the spokesman not only of the disciples but of the early church, most likely "had a rich vocabulary and a public speaker's flare for fresh creative expression."[1] This certainly shines in his letters.

Second, growing persecution could easily have limited the circulation of such a small letter. Nero's fires were heating up, and soon Rome would be aflame with religious hatred. Second Peter would, in fact, be Peter's last letter. Tradition records him being crucified upside-down—he chose this position because he did not feel worthy of dying the same way his Lord did—between A.D. 64 and 68.

---

1. Kenneth O. Gangel, "2 Peter," in *The Bible Knowledge Commentary*, New Testament edition, ed. John F. Walvoord and Roy B. Zuck (Wheaton, Ill.: Scripture Press Publications, Victor Books, 1983), p. 860.

Third, questions about Christ's return certainly did trouble people in the first century. Paul had to reassure the Thessalonians that the Day of the Lord had not already come (see 2 Thess. 2). And it seems that Peter had to deal with the opposite extreme: doubt that He *ever* would come (2 Pet. 3:3–10). Rather than seeing these ideas as contradictory, it is more logical to recognize them as two sides of the same coin.

Finally, as commentator Edwin A. Blum notes, "Authorship and canonicity were closely related," and church leaders "acknowledged 2 Peter to be Scripture because the evidence, both internal and external, showed its solid worth."[2]

Recipients

Unlike Peter's introduction in 1 Peter, the opening verses of 2 Peter do not give us any geographical details about his readers. From 2 Peter 3:1, though, we have reason to believe that he was writing to the same Jewish and Gentile Christians in Asia Minor that he wrote to in 1 Peter: "This is now, beloved, the second letter I am writing to you."

Purpose for Writing

The problem facing Christians in 1 Peter was persecution from the outside, but in 2 Peter it was poison from within. False teachers in the church were attempting to lead Christ's flock astray, denying Christ's lordship over them and taking away their hope of His return. They were promoting a very early form of Gnosticism, and Peter would have none of it. So his purpose, as Kenneth Gangel sums up,

> is to call Christians to spiritual growth so that they can combat apostasy as they look forward to the Lord's return.[3]

Structure of 2 Peter

We can divide Peter's second letter into three sections: (1) an

---

2. Edwin A. Blum, "2 Peter," in *The Expositor's Bible Commentary*, gen. ed. Frank E. Gaebelein (Grand Rapids, Mich.: Zondervan Publishing House, Regency Reference Library, 1981), vol. 12, p. 261. Blum provides an excellent, thorough treatment of the authorship debate in his introduction to 2 Peter (pp. 257–61).

3. Gangel, "2 Peter," p. 862.

exhortation to spiritual maturity (chap. 1), (2) a denunciation of false teachers (chap. 2), and (3) an encouragement to properly anticipate Christ's return (chap. 3).

Exhortation to Spiritual Maturity (Chap. 1)

In his opening words, Peter strikes at the heart of the Gnostic lie of a special, exclusive, elite knowledge of God. He reassures his readers that "the faith given them by God was of equal honor or privilege with that of the apostles' faith."[4]

> Simon Peter, a bond-servant and apostle of Jesus Christ,
> To those who have received a faith of the same kind as ours, by the righteousness of our God and Savior, Jesus Christ: Grace and peace be multiplied to you in the knowledge of God and of Jesus our Lord. (2 Pet. 1:1–2)

Indeed, Christ has "granted to us everything pertaining to life and godliness"—in other words, through knowing Him, we have everything we need for the spiritual life (v. 3). Note Peter's link to godliness here; it is a marked contrast to the false teachers' promotion of an immoral lifestyle. Peter sees God's "precious and magnificent promises" impacting us so that we can both partake of the holiness of the "divine nature" and escape "the corruption that is in the world by lust" (v. 4). For "faith" does not stand alone; real faith in God results in a changed life, which the ascending virtues in verses 5–7 illustrate.

> Now for this very reason also, applying all diligence, in your faith supply moral excellence, and in your moral excellence, knowledge, and in your knowledge, self-control, and in your self-control, perseverance, and in your perseverance, godliness, and in your godliness, brotherly kindness, and in your brotherly kindness, love.

If a person is growing in these qualities, he or she is a useful tool in God's hand, a lovely evidence of the goodness of knowing

4. Gangel, "2 Peter," p. 863.

Him (v. 8). If their lives are marked by the absence of these virtues, however, then they've closed their eyes to the fact that they have been washed clean from their sins and have returned to a dirty way of life (v. 9).

So Peter urges his readers to be diligent about making God's calling and choosing of them sure (v. 10). That is, "the genuineness of their profession will be demonstrated as they express these virtues."[5] Then they will be guaranteed to "receive a rich welcome into the eternal kingdom of our Lord and Savior Jesus Christ" (v. 11 NIV).

In light of what is at stake eternally, and knowing that his death is drawing near, Peter wants to keep these truths always in their minds (vv. 12–15). He assures them of their solid foundation of belief: his eyewitness account of Jesus not only in the flesh but transfigured into His glorified state (vv. 16–18). "This is My beloved Son with whom I am well-pleased" still rings in his ears— the God of heaven's very voice—and that voice is still heard just as surely in the words of His Scriptures, which proclaim the coming of His kingdom (vv. 19–21).

Denunciation of False Teachers (Chap. 2)

False prophets, however, unlike those who were moved unerringly by the Holy Spirit, will come up with ideas devoid of the Spirit of life and truth. Their "destructive heresies" will bring "swift destruction" on them (2:1). In the meantime, unfortunately, their corrupt teaching will lead many into corrupt behavior, bringing shame to "the way of the truth" (v. 2). They will be marked not by moral excellence but "sensuality" (v. 2), not by knowledge but "false words," and not by brotherly kindness but "greed" (v. 3a).

God's judgment, however, "is not idle, and their destruction is not asleep" (v. 3b). As surely as God has not spared the fallen angels, the wicked people in Noah's day, and the utterly depraved inhabitants of Sodom and Gomorrah, so He will not spare those who follow in their steps. And just as surely as He "preserved Noah" and "rescued righteous Lot," so He will rescue those walking in Christ's righteousness (vv. 4–10a). God is sovereign, His words are true, and He is in control.

---

5. Donald W. Burdick and John H. Skilton, note on 2 Peter 1:10, in *The NIV Study Bible*, ed. Kenneth L. Barker and others (Grand Rapids, Mich.: Zondervan Bible Publishers, 1985), p. 1899.

Peter then paints an unsparing portrait of the vile character of these false teachers (vv. 10b–19). Audacious, self-willed, blasphemous, ignorant, deceitful, adulterous, greedy, arrogant, seductive. They would be prophets for profit; promise freedom while they are themselves enslaved. It is a picture of misery—though they would paint over it with bright colors—which is why we don't always see them for what they are. So remember:

- False teachers are more interested in gaining popularity than in telling the truth.

- False teachers are more interested in getting than in giving.

- The personal life of a false teacher is a seduction to evil rather than an attraction to good.

- False teachers lead people away from God instead of closer to Him.

Peter says that a person who has known the way of freedom from sin and then rejects it for bondage is worse off than the one who never knew about freedom in the first place. For, like a sow who was washed but turns again to wallow in the mud, so those who turn their backs on righteousness and life have nowhere to go but to moral mire and spiritual death (vv. 20–22). To truly submit one's life to Christ means obeying Him as Lord.

Anticipation of Christ's Return (Chap. 3)

As if sitting up more in his seat and leaning toward his readers, Peter pauses to reiterate his purpose in writing to them.

> My dear friends, this is now the second time I've written to you, both letters reminders to hold your minds in a state of undistracted attention. Keep in mind what the holy prophets said, and the command of our Master and Savior that was passed on by your apostles.[6] (3:1–2)

Having urged them to ground themselves in the truth, Peter now warns them of "mockers" who will try to convince them that the Lord is not coming back for them (vv. 3–4). Though they say

6. Eugene H. Peterson, *The Message: The New Testament in Contemporary English* (Colorado Springs, Colo.: NavPress, 1993), p. 498.

that the world goes on just as it always has, Peter points out that the world hasn't always gone on—the Flood in Noah's time wiped out the world once before (vv. 5–6). And as surely as He destroyed the world in judgment before, so He will do it again—this time by fire, according to His promise (v. 7; see also Gen. 9:8–17).

For the Lord's judgment has not yet come—not because His promises are empty but because He wants as many who will to repent. His time frame is not our time frame, just as His ways are not our ways (2 Pet. 3:8–9; see also Isa. 55:8). He is a just judge, but He is also gracious and merciful.

The Day of the Lord will indeed come, Peter avers, and for those not ready it will come with the unwelcome surprise of a thief. Everything temporal will "be destroyed with intense heat, and the earth and its works will be burned up" (2 Pet. 3:10). Making this world their only world of concern, as the false teachers did, would be putting their hearts into pleasures that would not last.

Far better, Peter says, to put their efforts into the world that *will* last—the new heavens and new earth that God has promised, where "righteousness dwells" (vv. 11–13). This is the culmination of salvation history and the climactic conclusion to a story still in progress under divine direction. Because of this, they need to live in a new lifestyle appropriate to the new world, trusting that God's delay in judging wickedness is not an oversight but a testimony to His patient, saving work (vv. 14–15a).

Peter notes that "our beloved brother Paul" also teaches along these same lines—the apostles are unified in truth and purpose, exhorting Christ's followers to righteous living in light of the sureness of God's coming (vv. 15b–16a). Peter does confess, though, that some of the things Paul writes are a bit hard to understand; and those inclined to do so will distort his words, just as they distort the rest of Scripture to their own destruction (v. 16b).

With his warnings made and his encouragements given, Peter now wraps up his letter. Forewarned is forearmed, he seems to say; then he reveals the most powerful way to prepare their lives for eternity.

> You therefore, beloved, knowing this beforehand, be on your guard so that you are not carried away by the error of unprincipled men and fall from your own steadfastness, but grow in the grace and knowledge of our Lord and Savior Jesus Christ. To Him be the

glory, both now and to the day of eternity. Amen.
(vv. 17–18)

Grace and knowledge and glory—these are enough to transform any believer, even a humble fisherman, into a useful and faithful servant of our Lord and Savior, Jesus Christ.

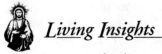 ## *Living Insights*

Let's revisit the beginning of Peter's letter and take a more personal look at those seven virtues that will help us lead productive lives for Christ.

To the foundation of our faith Peter would have us add "moral excellence" (1:5). How are you doing in this area? Are you walking in a manner worthy of your calling, pursuing holiness because God is holy? Are you a light of trustworthiness and dependability in the darkness of this unstable world?

_____

_____

_____

Next is "knowledge" (v. 5b). Are you getting to know Jesus and what pleases Him better? Are your relationships marked by understanding and insight? How strong is your appetite for the food of God's Word?

_____

_____

_____

Peter lists "self-control" after knowledge (v. 6a). If we know what God's will is, we will want to restrain those impulses that lead us away from Him. When you are tempted, especially sexually, do you turn the reins of your impulses over to the Holy Spirit?

_____

_____

_____

"Perseverance" follows self-control (v. 6b). How steadfast is your faith? When everyone else is heading in the opposite direction, do you stay with what you know to be true?

_____

_____

_____

Next comes "godliness" (v. 6c). How aware are you of God's presence in every aspect of your life? Does that awareness govern your actions, or do you tend to keep His reality at an arm's distance sometimes?

_____

_____

_____

After godliness comes "brotherly kindness" (v. 7). Does your awareness of God affect the way you treat others? Is kindness a quality that defines your life and shapes your behavior?

_____

_____

_____

Last, and at the peak of this list, is "love" (v. 7). Do you make it your aim to manifest Christ's love to all—even the guy who cuts you off on the freeway? Is loving others as Christ loves them usually at the forefront of your mind?

_____

_____

_____

David W. Gill says, "Christians must also 'make every effort' to grow ethically—that is, to grow from faith to love in a life that manifests God's truth."[7] Testifying to the reality of God—that's what these virtues do. And that's what we, as those called by Christ's name, are meant to do.

7. David W. Gill, *Peter the Rock: Extraordinary Insights from an Ordinary Man* (Downers Grove, Ill.: InterVarsity Press, 1986), p. 190.

Chapter 10

1 JOHN: GOD'S LIFE ON DISPLAY

A *Survey of 1 John*

Experienced hikers know that the best way to tell whether the water from a mountain stream is safe to drink is to follow it to its source and look for certain signs of purity. Is the water flowing or gathering into stagnant pools? Is it clean and clear or murky and contaminated?

These same kinds of tests can be applied to our lives as Christians, to see if we're a safe and pure reflection of the faith. And John's first letter gives us the signs to look for.

According to John, saying we know God isn't enough; the proof is in the living. As commentator David Jackman observes,

> To profess knowledge of God without a holy life, without a clean break with sin and a deep love for other Christians, is as much a delusion as to deny the incarnation of our Lord Jesus Christ. Belief and behavior are inseparable. Mind and heart belong together. True light leads to real love.[1]

What does God's life look like in a true believer? How can we recognize falseness in living and teaching that would try to lead us astray? John helps us answer these questions, but before we explore his letter, let's take a look at the situation that prompted it.

The Situation

John wrote his book around A.D. 90 from Ephesus, where he served as the overseer of the churches in Asia. Peter, Paul, and the other apostles had died at the hands of persecutors. Only John, who was perhaps in his eighties by now, remained as the last living link to the earthly ministry of Jesus.

---

1. David Jackman, *The Message of John's Letters: Living in the Love of God*, The Bible Speaks Today Series (Downers Grove, Ill.: InterVarsity Press, 1988), p. 16.

1 JOHN

	Walking with the God of Light		Responding to the God of Love			
	Living in the Light	**Staying in the Light**	**Practicing the Righteousness and Love of God**	**Testing the Spirits**	**Loving Others as God Loved Us**	**Believing in Jesus**
	CHAPTERS 1:5–2:11	CHAPTER 2:12–2:27	CHAPTERS 2:28–3:23	CHAPTERS 3:24–4:6	CHAPTER 4:7–21	CHAPTER 5
Fellowship with God Produces . . .	A clean life	A discerning life	A loving life			A confident life
Emphasis	Light	Truth	Love			Knowledge
Means	Obeying	Perceiving	Sacrificing			Believing
Christ	Advocate (2:1)	Holy One (2:20)	Son of God (3:8)		Savior of the World (4:14)	
Purposes	that we may have fellowship and joy (1:3–4)	that we may not sin (2:1)	that we may not be deceived (2:20)		that we may know that we have eternal life (5:13)	
Main Theme	Living in fellowship with God who is light and love					
Key Verses	1:5–7		4:10–16		5:11–13	

Prologue (1:1–4)

In this apostolic vacuum, false teachers had arisen who were claiming new insights into Christ and uprooting the apostles' teaching. John's goal was to call believers back to the foundation of their faith and to the essential task of following Jesus.

One source of the threat to the church was the Gnostics, who taught that matter was evil and only the spirit was good. Therefore, they denied the Incarnation, saying that the divine and holy Christ could not have had a material body. This belief spawned some strange theories: Some taught that Christ only *seemed* to be flesh and bone; while others taught that the divine Christ's spirit only entered into the man Jesus during His ministry and exited prior to the Cross because God couldn't suffer pain.

Denying that Jesus was God in the flesh led them to deny His atoning sacrifice, His redemption, and His offer of reconciliation with God. To the Gnostics, salvation came not by grace through faith but by freedom from the sinful body through mystical knowledge or *gnosis*, the root word of Gnostic.

They claimed that they alone possessed this higher, true knowledge of God. "They talked of being born of God," writes William Barclay, "of walking in the light, of having no sin, of dwelling in God, of knowing God."[2] They went so far as to form their own congregation, creating a spirit of elitism and drawing members from the main church (see 1 John 2:19).

The situation was serious. For the real effect of their false doctrines was "to eliminate the Christian ethic and to make fellowship within the Church impossible."[3] They were dismembering the body of Christ, sundering the unity of Jesus' church. And John meant to stop them.

John's Message

John's first epistle builds on the foundation he laid in his gospel. Just as that was written so we would believe (John 20:31), his letter was written so we can be confident in what we believe (1 John 5:13). He bases our assurance on the marks of true godliness, which are not philosophical and mysterious but practical and obvious.

John's main concern is that we know—really know—whether

2. William Barclay, *The Letters of John and Jude*, rev. ed., The Daily Study Bible Series (Philadelphia, Pa.: Westminster Press, 1976), p. 12.

3. Barclay, *The Letters of John and Jude*, p. 12.

we're on the right track with God.[4] When we are walking in fellowship with Him, we display His character and we have the confidence to reject any false teaching that would lead us away from Him.

The Structure of 1 John

Unlike Paul, John doesn't lay out his thoughts in a linear, point-by-point fashion. Instead, he orchestrates his subjects (including love and hate, life and death, light and darkness, truth and error) like themes in a symphony. He begins with a simple proposition then adds a contrasting idea. Then he weaves in new themes and new contrasts that crescendo and fall in waves. You can open his letter at any place and enjoy some variation on his basic message of believing rightly about God which results in behaving rightly in God.

Because John's style is dynamic and fluid, his letter is, as commentator Zane C. Hodges forthrightly admits, "notoriously difficult to outline."[5] One way to organize the text is in two movements based on John's two great proclamations about God: "God is Light" (1:5) and "God is love" (4:8). These attributes, in perfect balance, form the standards by which all Christian beliefs and behaviors are measured.

Prologue (1:1–4)

John's prologue touches on the opening themes of his gospel—Christ's preexistent presence as the Word with God from the beginning, and that Word becoming human to be seen and heard and touched by all (John 1:1–5, 14–18; 1 John 1:1–4). John gives his personal testimony about the realness of Jesus, the God-man; he was an eyewitness to the infinite in finite form (1 John 1:2–3a). Notice his verbs: he has "heard," he has "seen" with his own eyes, he has "looked at," he has "touched" with his own hands the Word of life (v. 1).

4. *Know* is an important word in the epistle, used forty times. It appears in Greek as *oida*, which means "to know absolutely," and *ginosko*, which emphasizes "knowledge by experience." See Glenn W. Barker, "1 John," in *The Expositor's Bible Commentary*, gen. ed. Frank E. Gaebelein (Grand Rapids, Mich.: Zondervan Publishing House, Regency Reference Library, 1981), vol. 12, p. 318. God has given every believer truths that we can know for certain and that we can confirm by our practice and experience.

5. Zane C. Hodges, "1 John," in *The Bible Knowledge Commentary*, New Testament edition, ed. John F. Walvoord and Roy B. Zuck (Wheaton, Ill.: Scripture Press Publications, Victor Books, 1983), p. 882.

What stronger refutation of the fantasies of Gnosticism can there be than John's firsthand experience of reality? And unlike the Gnostics, who are just "too far above" everyone else, John would have the greatest joy in experiencing true Christian fellowship with his readers (vv. 3b–4).

Walking with the God of Light (1:5–2:27)

John next reveals a basic principle about God that any sinful person who desires to have relationship with Him must recognize: "God is Light, and in Him there is no darkness at all" (v. 5). How can we who are born in darkness walk with God who is Light?

Living in the Light (1:5–2:11)

To live in the light, we must first reject three false claims about our condition before God: (1) that we can fellowship with God and still live in sin (v. 6), (2) that we're not sinners by nature (v. 8), and (3) that we have not sinned (v. 10).[6]

Each of these claims denies the truth about who we are and what we've done. The solution for denial, John says, is confession. Admitting our sins opens the door for God to forgive us. Forgiveness leads to cleansing, and cleansing makes us fit for fellowship with Him (vv. 7, 9).

God welcomes us into His presence on the basis of the atoning sacrifice of Christ (2:1). As our Advocate, or mediating priest, Jesus Christ offered Himself on the cross as "the propitiation for our sins; and not for ours only, but also for those of the whole world" (v. 2). The word *propitiation* means "to appease," and "it includes the idea of turning away the wrath of God from the sinner to the substitute."[7] To be saved, we must put our faith in Jesus as our substitutionary atonement for sin.

To identify those who truly have faith in Christ, John tells us to see if they "keep His commandments" (vv. 3, 5) and "walk in the same manner as He walked" (v. 6). We all slip up morally, though. Are we still saved even if we occasionally sin? Yes, says David Jackman.

> We have already learned that no Christian can claim to be without sin in this life. That sort of perfection

6. See Jackman, *The Message of John's Letters*, pp. 29, 33.

7. Jackman, *The Message of John's Letters*, p. 45.

waits for heaven. But we have a goal, which defines our present direction, and for all of us much more progress towards that goal is always possible. It is the direction in which our life is travelling which determines whether or not our Christian profession is genuine.[8]

The more we abide in Christ, the more we love people as He loved them; and the more we love, the more we live in the light (v. 10).

Staying in the Light (2:12-27)

In this section, John encourages his readers that their sins are forgiven, that they know God, and that they are overcoming the Evil One (vv. 12-14). But he also cautions them about a couple of spiritual dangers so they will stay walking in the light.

First, he warns them not to love the world, for loving the world steals their affection from God (v. 15). The things of the world—power, fame, fortune—appeal to our lusts, which are not of God. The entire corrupt system will one day fade away like a star that burns brightly then disappears into darkness. Only those who pursue the will of God will live with Him forever (vv. 16-17).

Second, John warns his readers about false teachers. He calls them "antichrists," who, like *the* Antichrist, claim to teach the truth but actually deceive people (vv. 18-19). Their real colors appear when they deny that Jesus is the Messiah (vv. 22-23). John tells his readers that they already have the Holy Spirit, who helps them know what is true (vv. 20-21). He encourages them to abide in the original teachings of the apostles and in Jesus Himself, who has given them the Spirit as their Teacher (vv. 24-27).

Responding to the God of Love (2:28-5:21)

In his second movement, John turns to the sublime subject of God's love and how we demonstrate His love in our lives.

Practicing the Righteousness and Love of God (2:28-3:23)

Out of His great love for us, God has called us to be His children, and one day, He will transform us completely into the likeness of His Son (2:28-3:2). Until then, we are to grow in His likeness,

---

8. Jackman, *The Message of John's Letters*, pp. 42-43.

maturing in righteousness and shunning sin (3:3–7).

The children of the devil are easy to spot because they act like their father. In the same way, it should be easy to identify the children of God because they practice the righteousness of their Father. Again, John isn't implying perfection; he's simply saying that true believers don't maintain a lifestyle of sin, because God's seed (the Holy Spirit) has been planted in them (vv. 8–10).

As children of the God who is love, the greatest way we resemble our Father is by loving His children. Hating our brothers and sisters is as deadly as Cain's hatred for Abel (vv. 11–15). Our example is Christ, who sacrificed Himself for the sake of others (v. 16). His act was real, meeting us at our deepest need. And it was active, reaching out and changing our situation. We, too, are called to a seeing, reaching, active love that makes a difference, as John next makes clear.

> Whoever has the world's goods, and sees his brother in need and closes his heart against him, how does the love of God abide in him? Little children, let us not love with word or with tongue, but in deed and truth. (vv. 17–18)

Expressing God's love to others benefits us as well. It confirms that we are His and pours confidence into our faith. Our prayers ring with the security and assurance of an obedient child before a loving Father: "whatever we ask we receive from Him" (vv. 19–23).

Testing the Spirits (3:24–4:6)

In 3:24, John introduces the role of the Spirit in our assurance. Just as we can tell the children of God from the children of the devil by their deeds, so we can discern God's Spirit from false spirits by what they confess. Whether it's cult members at your door or preachers on television, if they deny that Jesus Christ came in the flesh, they are not from God. They are counterfeits and are from "the world." We don't have to fear them, because "greater is He who is in you than he who is in the world" (v. 4b).

Loving as God Loves (4:7–21)

Circling back to the theme of love, John tells us, "Beloved, let us love one another" (v. 7a). Many spiritual leaders have taught this ideal, but John goes further and gives us the moral reason for love—which is rooted in the Person of God:

> For love is from God; and everyone who loves is
> born of God and knows God. The one who does not
> love does not know God, for God is love. (vv. 7b–8)

Everything God does, He does in love because He *is* love. The climactic demonstration of His love came when He sent His own Son to die for us on the cross (vv. 9–10).

"If God so loved us," John reasons, "we also ought to love one another" (v. 11). Our love for others flows out of God's love for us. As we love others, *we* display the reflection of our Father (v. 12). The Spirit He has given us, our confession of Jesus as His Son, and our love for others all combine to reassure us of our oneness with God: "we abide in Him and He in us" (vv. 13–16).

This loving fellowship with God gives us confidence in the day of judgment, for His love casts out all our fears of punishment (vv. 17–18). The end of the matter is this: loving God and loving others is a package deal. You can't have one without the other (vv. 19–21).

Believing in Jesus (5:1–21)

John concludes his letter on a note of faith, for faith is the key to overcoming the world and its lies. The *essential tenet* of our faith is "that Jesus is the Christ" (5:1). The *evidence* of our faith is our love for others, love for God, and obedience to God's commands (v. 2). The *outcome* of faith is victory over the world (vv. 4–5). And the *confirmation* of our faith is the testimony of the Spirit (vv. 6–10).

John plants his readers on the solid bedrock of God's eternal promise:

> And the testimony is this, that God has given us
> eternal life, and this life is in His Son. He who has
> the Son has the life; he who does not have the Son
> does not have the life. These things I have written
> to you who believe in the name of the Son of God,
> so that you may know that you have eternal life.
> (vv. 11–13)

This sure footing gives us confidence in our prayers (vv. 14–15), confidence in helping others out of sin (vv. 16–17), confidence against the Evil One (v. 18), confidence against world forces (v. 19), and confidence in our relationship with God (v. 20).

The letter ends with a warning: "Little children, guard yourselves from idols" (v. 21). What idols is John talking about? He might have in mind the carved figures that most of his readers worshiped before coming to Christ. But he's probably thinking in broader terms. An idol can be anything in the Christian's life that elbows God out of center place in our lives. Modern idols can be money, material goods, power, people, or fame. They can be "false ideas of God," writes David Jackman,

> cardboard cut-out substitutes for the living and true God, that invade and destroy our spiritual lives. Whether it is the "demythologized" God of radical theology, shorn of his supernatural power, or the pocket-size God of evangelical over-familiarity, deprived of his majesty, the danger is the same. We can all too easily think we have him sewn up, we know all about him, we can predict his responses and even condition them. But what we have is not God. It is an idol of our own making, a thinly veiled excuse for worshipping ourselves.[9]

The opposite of idolatry is faith in Christ—complete, utter dependence on the One who offers us eternal life and invites us into personal fellowship with a God who is pure light and unfailing love.

 Living Insights

First John is built on the premise that God changes people. His light penetrates our defenses, and His love turns us around and heads us in a new direction—toward Himself. From John's epistle, we can glean four traits that will increasingly characterize us as we grow in our fellowship with God: a clean life (1:5–2:11), a discerning life (2:12–27), a loving life (2:28–4:21), and a confident life (5:1–21).

How are you progressing on the road to a clean life? Sometimes we can convince ourselves that our "little" offenses don't affect our walk with God. But John says that all sin matters to Him, so we

---

9. Jackman, *The Message of John's Letters*, p. 172.

must take it seriously. Are there any sins you need to bring out of the shadows and into the scrutiny of God's light?

_____

_____

_____

How well are you doing on your way to a discerning life? What voices of authority are you listening to? Are any of them leading you into spiritual tangents, away from the truth about Christ?

_____

_____

_____

How about a loving life? Take a moment to read 1 John 3:11–18. Is there a needy person in your circle of relationships? How can you open your heart and hands to them?

_____

_____

_____

Finally, are you striding toward a confident life? The world and its false teachers will fill your head with doubts. *Am I loved? Do I matter? Am I wasting my life by following God?* John wrote his letter with one main goal in mind: to give you confidence in God. As you browse 1 John 5, what promise does God seem to give directly to you to build your faith in Him?

_____

_____

_____

Chapter 11

2 JOHN: A LETTER
TO A LADY

A Survey of 2 John

T
he two most difficult things to get straight in life," Eugene
Peterson writes, "are love and God. More often than not, the
mess people make of their lives can be traced to failure or stupidity
or meanness in one or both of these areas."[1]

Is it any wonder, then, that John had to write about these topics
not once, not twice, but three times?

In his second epistle, John corrects a loving "lady" whose hospitality may have actually been harming the cause of the Gospel.
Lacking discernment, she had allowed her love to spill over the
boundaries of truth—the truth about God revealed in Jesus Christ.
And when the borders of the truth get washed away, people are set
adrift in dangerous waters rather than moved from death to life.

Love cannot be separated from the truth. And neither can truth
be separated from love. Let's journey with John as he clarifies these
twin themes and find our way to safety and balance.

The Writer

John identifies himself only as "the elder," which can refer to
his age or his religious office—or both. As the sole surviving apostle,
John was a highly esteemed and well-loved patriarch of the churches
in Asia. His gentle language and pastoral style indelibly mark this
letter, which is perhaps why he didn't have to sign his name—the
people knew he was the author.[2] As a modern clergyman might
sign a letter to his congregation simply, "Your Pastor," the omission
of John's name actually lends intimacy and warmth to his message.

This chapter has been adapted from "A Postcard to a Lady and Her Kids," from the study
guide *New Testament Postcards*, coauthored by Ken Gire and Bryce Klabunde, from the Bible-
teaching ministry of Charles R. Swindoll (Anaheim, Calif.: Insight for Living, 1996),
pp. 10–17.

1. Eugene H. Peterson, *The Message: The New Testament in Contemporary English* (Colorado
Springs, Colo.: NavPress, 1993), p. 500.

2. Also, 2 John may have come in a bundle of letters to the church, making a more specific
address unnecessary. Perhaps, too, John wanted to protect himself and his readers from
persecution should the letter fall into the wrong hands.

2 JOHN

	Introduction	Walk in Truth and Love!	Stand Against Error!	Conclusion
	Greeting Affirmation Encouragement	The lady's children The lady herself Love one another; walk in obedience	The circumstance (many deceivers) The warning ("Watch yourselves!") The instruction (strong but necessary)	Personal Farewell
	VERSES 1–3	VERSES 4–6	VERSES 7–11	VERSES 12–13
Emphasis	Encouragement to love and affirm		Exhortation to be discerning	
Tone	Gracious	Concerned	Strong	Warm
Personal Touch	"I love you" (implied, v. 1)	"I ask you" (v. 5)	"I warn you" (implied, v. 8)	"I hope to come to you" (v. 12)
Main Theme	Loving others within the limits that truth allows			
Key Verses	Verses 5–6			

The Recipients

He addresses his brief words to "the chosen lady and her children." Bible scholars debate whether the "lady" and "children" are actual people or metaphors for the church and its members. Elsewhere in the New Testament, the church is personified as a woman (see Eph. 5:22–32; Rev. 19:7), and John often spoke to his readers as "children" (see 1 John 2:1, 12, 13, 18, 28; 3:1, 2, 7, 10, 18; 4:4; 5:2, 21). However, personal references, such as "lady" (2 John 5), her "house" (v. 10), and her "sister" (v. 13) could indicate that John is writing to a literal woman. This latter approach is the one we will take.

Like Lydia in the book of Acts (see 16:14–15, 40), this lady of 2 John was a gracious hostess, opening her home for the sake of the ministry. Her love flowed freely to anyone who knocked on her door, including the traveling teachers and prophets who came to town.

The Situation

Before the New Testament was complete, Christians depended on itinerant prophets and teachers to communicate the divine truth they needed to build their faith. They revered these traveling preachers, often housing and feeding them in the finest style they could afford. Unfortunately, not all the roving reverends were worthy of such warm hospitality. It was not uncommon for fraudulent men to exploit the trusting Christians. Even the secular writers attested to their abuses:

> Lucian, the Greek writer, in his work called the *Peregrinus*, draws the picture of a man who had found the easiest possible way of making a living without working. He was an itinerant charlatan who lived on the fat of the land by travelling round the various communities of the Christians, settling down wherever he liked and living luxuriously at their expense.[3]

The problem was so widespread that strict rules were eventually laid down in *The Didache*, or "The Teaching," an early book of

---

3. William Barclay, *The Letters of John and Jude*, rev. ed., The Daily Study Bible Series (Philadelphia, Pa.: Westminster Press, 1976), pp. 133–34.

church order. Certain indicators were listed as red flags. For example, if the person stayed for more than three days; if he asked for money while speaking "in the Spirit"; or if, when he decided to settle down, he refused to work—this teacher was not to be trusted. As the document bluntly states, "He is a Christmonger: of such men beware."[4]

John had heard that some of these insidious "Christmongers" were welcomed into this woman's home. Naively, she was taking them in, not realizing that by doing so she was helping spread heresy. While affirming her charitable spirit, John sends her an urgent message: *Make sure your love supports the truth.*

The Letter

John's epistle can be divided into four sections: an introduction (2 John 1–3), exhortations to walk in truth and love (vv. 4–6), instruction to stand against error (vv. 7–11), and a conclusion (vv. 12–13).

Introduction (vv. 1–3)

At the outset, John expresses his deep feelings for his readers:

> The elder to the chosen lady and her children,
> whom I love in truth; and not only I, but also all
> who know the truth, for the sake of the truth which
> abides in us and will be with us forever. (vv. 1–2)

His love for this lady and her children is grounded "in truth." It is proper. It is pure. It reflects the reality of Christ. And he writes "for the sake of the truth," which is as eternal as God.

In verse 3, John bestows God's blessing on his readers:

> Grace, mercy and peace will be with us, from God
> the Father and from Jesus Christ, the Son of the
> Father, in truth and love.

The blessings of grace, mercy, and peace flow out of the Father and the Son by means of truth and love. In the same way, truth and love must be the channel through which we bless others.

---

4. As quoted in Barclay, *The Letters of John and Jude*, p. 134.

Exhortations (vv. 4–6)

John next commends the lady's children.

> I was very glad to find some of your children
> walking in truth, just as we have received command-
> ment to do from the Father. (v. 4)

Notice, only *some* are walking in truth. Apparently, others are
straying from it—and that's where the problems lie.

In verses 5–6, John reminds this lady to love others—but in
the way Christ prescribed, "according to His commandments" (v. 6).

> Now I ask you, lady, not as though I were writing
> to you a new commandment, but the one which we
> have had from the beginning, that we love one an-
> other. And this is love, that we walk according to
> His commandments. This is the commandment, just
> as you have heard from the beginning, that you
> should walk in it.

Love does not contradict the commandments of Scripture. In
fact, as the apostle Paul wrote,

> Owe nothing to anyone except to love one an-
> other; for he who loves his neighbor has fulfilled the
> law. For this, "You shall not commit adultery, You
> shall not murder, You shall not steal, You shall not
> covet," and if there is any other commandment, it
> is summed up in this saying, "You shall love your
> neighbor as yourself." Love does no wrong to a
> neighbor; therefore love is the fulfillment of the law.
> (Rom. 13:8–10)

True love never compromises its standards. Never consents to
sin. Rather, it leads us and those we care about closer to Christ.

Instruction (vv. 7–11)

And it is Christ, and the accuracy of His Gospel, that should
be our primary concern.

> For many deceivers have gone out into the
> world, those who do not acknowledge Jesus Christ
> as coming in the flesh. This is the deceiver and the
> antichrist. Watch yourselves, that you do not lose

what we have accomplished, but that you may receive a full reward. Anyone who goes too far and does not abide in the teaching of Christ, does not have God; the one who abides in the teaching, he has both the Father and the Son. (2 John 7–9)

Although these teachers (apparently Gnostics) spoke respectfully of Christ, they denied the truth about Him and were thus really against Him and His teaching—"anti-Christ." They went beyond Christ's teaching, adding their own ideas and twisting His words. As a result, they had no part in God, and God had no part in them.

By showing love to these false teachers, the lady was, in fact, aiding the enemy. This is why John says,

If anyone comes to you and does not bring this teaching, do not receive him into your house, and do not give him a greeting; for the one who gives him a greeting participates in his evil deeds. (vv. 10–11)

Taking these verses out of context, some Christians have used them to justify the most unloving behavior. John isn't telling us to slam the door in the face of everyone who disagrees with us. In his mind are false teachers who slip into our churches with their heresies about Christ and cause people to stumble in their faith. To receive them is to become partners in their crime. The most loving thing to do—for our sake and the sake of those we care about—is to draw a line and stand firm in the truth.

Conclusion (vv. 12–13)

With his characteristic warmth, John concludes his letter with hope and joy.

Though I have many things to write to you, I do not want to do so with paper and ink; but I hope to come to you and speak face to face, so that your joy may be made full.
The children of your chosen sister greet you. (vv. 12–13)

In a day of relativism and tolerance, John's briefest letter sounds the loudest wake-up call. Be courageous! Stand for what God says is right! Telling someone the truth may be difficult, but, in the long run, it is the most loving thing to do.

Living Insights

Our society would have us think that if we truly love people, we'll accept them regardless of their beliefs. This is called "tolerance." Yet what kind of love lets someone believe a lie that eventually destroys them? That's not love; that's indifference, the opposite of love.

To really care for someone is to tell him or her the truth—not in a demeaning way but with gentleness and respect. Love and truth, as commentator John Stott explains, must exist in balance.

> Our love is not to be so blind as to ignore the views and conduct of others. Truth should make our love discriminating. . . . On the other hand, we must never champion the truth in a harsh or bitter spirit. . . . So the Christian fellowship should be marked equally by love and truth, and we are to avoid the dangerous tendency to extremism, pursuing either at the expense of the other. Our love grows soft if it is not strengthened by truth, and our truth grows hard if it is not softened by love. We need to live according to Scripture which commands us both to love each other in the truth and to hold the truth in love.[5]

Do you know someone who has placed his or her faith in a lie? If so, have you found it difficult to speak the truth in love to this person? The place to begin is to thoroughly know the truth yourself. Study the following chart on the essentials of the faith, and get to know their scriptural basis. Then jot down some thoughts concerning what truth this person needs to hear. Someone once said, "The man who loved me the most told me the truth." How about you? Are you willing to love that much?

5. J. R. W. Stott, *The Epistles of John: An Introduction and Commentary*, The Tyndale New Testament Commentaries (Grand Rapids, Mich.: William B. Eerdmans Publishing Co., 1960), pp. 204–5.

Essentials of the Faith	Scriptural Sources
Inerrancy of Scripture	2 Tim. 3:16; 2 Pet. 1:21
Virgin birth and deity of Christ	Isa. 7:14; Matt. 1:18–26; Luke 1:26–38; John 1:1, 14; 8:53–58; Col. 1:15–20
Sinless nature of Christ	2 Cor. 5:21; Heb. 4:15; 7:26; 1 Pet. 2:21–22; 1 John 3:5
Sinful nature of humanity	Rom. 3:10–18, 23
Substitutionary death of the Savior	Rom. 5:6–8; 2 Cor. 5:21
Effectiveness of Christ's blood to cleanse sin	Heb. 1:3; 9:26; 1 John 1:7, 9
Bodily resurrection of Christ	Luke 24:36–43; Rom. 6:3–6; 1 Cor. 15:1–11
Ascension of Christ and His present ministry	Acts 1:6–9; Eph. 4:7–10; John 14:1–3; Rom. 8:34
Literal, future return of Christ to the earth	Matt. 24; John 14:3; Acts 1:11; 2 Thess. 1:6–10; Rev. 1:7

_____

_____

_____

_____

_____

_____

_____

_____

_____

_____

_____

Chapter 12

3 JOHN: THREE MEN IN A CHURCH

A Survey of 3 John

In many respects, 3 John bears a striking resemblance to 2 John. They are about the same length, were written about the same time, address the issue of the church's attitude toward traveling teachers, and are anchored to the themes of truth and love.

However, as commentator David Jackman observes, the epistles are alike but opposite—as opposite as your right hand from your left hand.

> Whereas 2 John is primarily a warning against welcoming "deceivers," 3 John is a warning against rejecting those who are true fellow Christians and ambassadors of the gospel. It is the positive complement of the negative prohibitions of 2 John, reminding Gaius and his congregation that the possible abuse of hospitality by the heretics is not to become an excuse for failing to show hospitality to true and faithful Christian preachers.[1]

The contrasts between the two letters are just as striking as the resemblances. In 2 John, a lady was receiving the wrong kind of travelers; in 3 John, a man was shunning the right kind of travelers. In 2 John, it was a matter of misplaced hospitality; in 3 John, it was a matter of missing hospitality. In 2 John, truth was needed to balance love; in 3 John, love was needed to balance truth.

Three Different Men

John's third letter focuses on three men. The first is Gaius, the recipient of the letter and a close friend of John's. He was gracious,

---

This chapter is adapted from "A Postcard of Candid Truth," from the study guide *New Testament Postcards*, coauthored by Ken Gire and Bryce Klabunde, from the Bible-teaching ministry of Charles R. Swindoll (Anaheim, Calif.: Insight for Living, 1996), pp. 18–24.

1. David Jackman, *The Message of John's Letters: Living in the Love of God* (Downers Grove, Ill.: InterVarsity Press, 1988), p. 190.

3 JOHN

	Encouragement of Gaius	Confrontation of Diotrephes	Affirmation of Demetrius	Conclusion
	Sickly (?) / Obedient / Hospitable / Loving / Supportive	Proud / Rigid and negative / Accusing / "Church boss" complex	Good testimony / Community / Scriptures / John	Letter is abbreviated / John hopes to visit / Shalom!
	VERSES 1–8	VERSES 9–11	VERSE 12	VERSES 13–14
Tone	Confirming	Denunciating	Endorsing	
Relationships	To the truth of God	With other Christians	In the world	
Emphasis	Keep it up!	Stop it!	Good for you!	
Paraphrase	"I love you, and I pray for you" (vv. 1–2)	"I call attention to your deeds" (v. 10)	"I hear good things about him" (v. 12)	
Main Theme	Holding to the truth with a loving attitude			
Key Verse	"Beloved, do not imitate what is evil, but what is good. The one who does good is of God; the one who does evil has not seen God." (v. 11)			

107

generous, and kind, always willing to open his arms to outsiders in need.

The second is Diotrephes, the lay leader causing problems. According to commentator John Stott, his name "means 'Zeus-reared, nursling of Zeus' and was only to be found 'in noble and ancient families.'"[2] Despite Diotrephes' apparently noble bloodline, he possessed a rather ignoble temperament. He was domineering, inhospitable, exclusive, and proud.

The third man is Demetrius, who was possibly the messenger who delivered the letter and might have had the important job of representing John before Gaius and Diotrephes.

Three Different Needs

These three names form a natural outline for 3 John: Gaius is the recipient of *encouragement* (vv. 1–8); Diotrephes is the object of *confrontation* (vv. 9–11); and Demetrius is the subject of *affirmation* (v. 12).

Encouragement of Gaius (vv. 1–8)

John's first concern is to bolster the confidence of his friend Gaius.

> The elder to the beloved Gaius, whom I love in truth.
> Beloved, I pray that in all respects you may prosper and be in good health, just as your soul prospers.
> (vv. 1–2)

Four times John calls Gaius "beloved"—twice here and twice in verses 5 and 11. John's friendship with Gaius is based "in truth," that is, the truth of the Gospel which unites all believers in Christ.

John prays that Gaius will prosper physically just as he is prospering spiritually. Perhaps his prayer is a response to reports that Gaius is sick. It is a testament to Gaius' spiritual growth, however, that John would want his body to be as well as his soul. And John can't conceal his parental pride in Gaius' progress in the faith:

> For I was very glad when brethren came and testified
> to your truth, that is, how you are walking in truth.

2. J. R. W. Stott, *The Epistles of John: An Introduction and Commentary*, The Tyndale New Testament Commentaries Series (Grand Rapids, Mich.: William B. Eerdmans Publishing Co., 1960), p. 225.

I have no greater joy than this, to hear of my children walking in the truth. (vv. 3–4)

Gaius is the kind of person who weighs each word, each decision, each action on the scale of Christ's higher standards. He is faithful in truth—the first requirement of a good disciple. He also is faithful in love:

> Beloved, you are acting faithfully in whatever you accomplish for the brethren, and especially when they are strangers; and they have testified to your love before the church. You will do well to send them on their way in a manner worthy of God. For they went out for the sake of the Name, accepting nothing from the Gentiles. Therefore we ought to support such men, so that we may be fellow workers with the truth. (vv. 5–8)

With his grid of truth, Gaius is able to discern the genuineness of these traveling preachers. Then, with arms of love, he helps them "in a manner worthy of God" (v. 6). They were ministers for the sake of Christ—emissaries for the King of Kings. John says that when we support such people, we become "fellow workers with the truth" (v. 8). We become partakers "with what the truth accomplishes in people's hearts and lives."[3]

Unlike Gaius, however, Diotrephes "is more interested in furthering his own position than in furthering the work of God."[4]

Confrontation of Diotrephes (vv. 9–11)

Just as John revealed the light in Gaius, he turns to expose the darkness in Diotrephes:

> I wrote something to the church; but Diotrephes, who loves to be first among them, does not accept what we say. For this reason, if I come, I will call attention to his deeds which he does, unjustly accusing us with wicked words; and not satisfied

3. Zane C. Hodges, "3 John," in *The Bible Knowledge Commentary*, New Testament edition, ed. John F. Walvoord and Roy B. Zuck (Wheaton, Ill.: Scripture Press Publications, Victor Books, 1983), p. 913.

4. Glenn W. Barker, "3 John," in *The Expositor's Bible Commentary*, gen. ed. Frank E. Gaebelein (Grand Rapids, Mich.: Zondervan Publishing House, Regency Reference Library, 1981), vol. 12, p. 375.

with this, he himself does not receive the brethren, either, and he forbids those who desire to do so and puts them out of the church. (vv. 9–10)

Whatever letter John had written to the church no longer exists, probably because Diotrephes destroyed it. He views the church as "his turf," and he is determined to keep it that way. He has not only rejected John's teaching and apostolic authority, he has falsely accused the apostle and bolted the door against his messengers. He has even gone so far as to excommunicate anyone in the church who received them. Instead of truth, Diotrephes spreads lies; instead of love, he spreads fear.

What would cause a leader to become so jealous and defensive? It wasn't a matter of doctrinal differences. In verse 9, John puts his finger on the core problem: Diotrephes "loves to be first." From that brief sketch unfolds the entire sordid picture.

Concerning Diotrephes and all the leaders like him throughout church history, David Jackman writes:

> Destroying unity, flaunting authority, making up his own rules to safeguard his position, spreading lies about those whom he had designated his enemies, cutting off other Christians on suspicion of guilt by association—the catalogue is appalling. This is what happens when someone who loves to be first decides to use the church to satisfy his inner longing for a position of pre-eminence, for his own personal aggrandisement. We do not know whether or not Diotrephes had any official position, or whether he simply used the force of his personality to swing things his way. Either was possible and still is. There are churches today which are in the pocket of one person, or one family dynasty. Nothing can happen without the approval of Mr. X, because it is "his" church. Consequently, in effect, there can be no biblical plurality of eldership, no fresh or innovative ideas, no forward movement or spiritual growth. The Holy Spirit has long ago been drummed out of office in a church like that, where "Diotrephes" rules. What a travesty of the Christian faith and family![5]

5. Jackman, *The Message of John's Letters*, p. 198.

It isn't long before an outbreak of "Diotrephes' disease" breeds a whole congregation of self-willed, prideful followers. The doors of ministry close, and the body dies. It's a sad fate for any church. That's why John pleads with Gaius to guard himself against the evil disease and continue doing good:

> Beloved, do not imitate what is evil, but what is good. The one who does good is of God; the one who does evil has not seen God. (v. 11)

John gives Gaius an opportunity to do what is right by receiving Demetrius, a good man who deserves a good welcome.

Affirmation of Demetrius (v. 12)

Perhaps Demetrius is one of the "brethren" whom Diotrephes has cold-shouldered (see v. 10). John, however, gives him the warmest endorsement:

> Demetrius has received a good testimony from everyone, and from the truth itself; and we add our testimony, and you know that our testimony is true. (v. 12)

It is critical for John to keep the lines of communication open between himself and this troubled church. So he sends his best man, Demetrius, with three impressive references. First, everyone Demetrius knows vouches for him; second, his life lines up with the truth, which testifies on his behalf; and third, John gives him his personal stamp of approval.

Words of Farewell (vv. 13–14)

If nothing else, John's brief letter shows us that the early church had the same kinds of problems our churches have today. Yet, in spite of their conflicts, the ministries went on. God uses cracked, failure-prone vessels to feed a spiritually starving world (see 2 Cor. 4:7).

In the final verses of his letter, John expresses a deep desire to visit Gaius. Until he arrives, he prays for God's peace to settle on the church.

> I had many things to write to you, but I am not willing to write them to you with pen and ink; but I hope to see you shortly, and we will speak face to face.

Peace be to you. The friends greet you. Greet
the friends by name. (3 John 13–14)

Every church has at least one Diotrephes, who will try to cast
a gray shadow across the ministry—unjustly accusing leaders, shut-
ting out people in need, intimidating church members. Emerging
from the cloud is a Gaius or Demetrius, who displays a rainbow of
virtues—hospitality, generosity, integrity, and purity. Follow these
examples, because they bear the marks of those who walk in truth.

 Living Insights
_____

Diotrephes' pride took over his life in stages. The first stage was
resistance: he refused to submit to authority by not accepting John's
teaching (3 John 9). Second was *criticism*: he started hurling unjust
accusations at those in authority (v. 10a). Third was *isolation*: he
shut himself off from outside instruction and correction—he didn't
"receive the brethren" (v. 10b). Fourth was *control*: he forbade the
people from listening to any teaching except his own (v. 10c).

Maybe you've seen others follow this downward path; or perhaps
you're in one of those stages now. Shine the following questions
into your heart. What signs of pride do you see?

Am I resisting legitimate authority?

_____

_____

Do I have a critical spirit?

_____

_____

Have I isolated myself from people who might instruct or correct
me?

_____

_____

Am I controlling people with intimidation or threats?

_____

What warnings do the following Proverbs call out to you about the dangers of pride?

Proverbs 11:2 _____

_____

Proverbs 13:10 _____

_____

Proverbs 16:5, 18 _____

_____

Proverbs 29:1 _____

_____

Jesus prescribes a cure for "Diotrephes' disease" in His teaching against the Pharisees and scribes. According to Matthew 23:1–12, what are His instructions?

_____

_____

_____

How can you put Christ's remedy into action?

_____

_____

Chapter 13

JUDE: MANUAL FOR SURVIVAL

A *Survey of Jude*

"Fight for the faith!"

These words resonate like a battle cry in Jude's brief but powerful epistle. Like an experienced field commander, Jude rallies the troops to stand firm against false doctrine and defend the truth of Christ.

The threat came from a group of false teachers who were promoting heresies similar to those we studied in John's epistles. Claiming spiritual insights beyond what Christ and the apostles taught, these apostates had slipped into the congregation and were amassing a following with their persuasive lies. Their divide-and-conquer mission was weakening the church and spreading confusion among the new believers.

Jude commands his readers to find their voices and proclaim the truth. To come to the aid of the weak. To fight for their beliefs. To contend earnestly for the faith.

Author and Audience

Jude introduces himself as "a bond-servant of Jesus Christ, and brother of James" (Jude 1a). This James is the same man who wrote the book of James, and both of them were Jesus' half brothers (see Matt. 13:55; Mark 6:3).[1] Why didn't Jude list his kinship with Jesus? Most likely, modesty and reverence constrained him from boasting in it. But also, he was more than a brother of Jesus; he was a disciple—which is a stronger tie than blood (see Luke 8:19–21).

He addresses his letter "to those who are the called, beloved in God the Father, and kept for Jesus Christ" (v. 1b). Because of his

This chapter is adapted from "The Acts of the Apostates," "Why Bother to Battle?" and "Get Your Act Together!" in the study guide *New Testament Postcards*, coauthored by Ken Gire and Bryce Klabunde, from the Bible-teaching ministry of Charles R. Swindoll (Anaheim, Calif.: Insight for Living, 1996), pp. 25–48.

1. We say "half brother" because, although James, Jude, and Jesus shared the same mother, Mary, Jesus had a heavenly Father.

JUDE

	Greeting and Purpose	Exposure of False Teachers	Warnings and Commands to Christians	Benediction
	Mercy, peace and love **What to do:** Contend for the faith! **Why:** Certain persons have secretly slipped in . . .	Doom is certain Guilt is sure Spirituality is empty Lives are godless	"Remember!" (verse 17) "Keep yourselves!" (verse 21) "Have mercy!" (verse 22) "Save!" (verse 23)	Our ultimate hope Our infinite God
	VERSES 1–4	*VERSES 5–16*	*VERSES 17–23*	*VERSES 24–25*
Emphasis	Appealing	Revealing	Reminding	Praising
Tone	Personal concern	Bold exposure	Strong exhortation	Great hope
Directed to	Those *"beloved in God the Father"* (v. 1)	Those who *"indulged in gross immorality"* (v. 7)	*"But you, beloved . . . "* (vv. 17, 20)	*"The only God"* (v. 25)
Main Theme	Exposing false teachers and standing firm in the faith			
Key Verses	"Contend earnestly for the faith" (v. 3b); verses 21–23			

many references to the Old Testament and Jewish literature, Jude was probably speaking to Jewish Christians. In a broader sense, though, his letter is to all of us, for every believer is "called" by the Spirit, "beloved" by the Father, and "kept" safe in Christ.

Similarities to 2 Peter

As you read the book of Jude, you might notice a striking resemblance to 2 Peter. The two books describe the false teachers in very similar terms and refer to the same Old Testament stories (see Jude 4–18 and 2 Pet. 2:1–3:4). It's obvious that one author borrowed from the other, but Bible scholars are divided over who copied whom. A comparison of the two epistles reveals that Peter probably wrote first. According to commentators Bruce Wilkinson and Kenneth Boa, Peter

> anticipates the future rise of apostate teachers (2 Pet. 2:1–2; 3:3) while Jude records the historical fulfillment of Peter's words (vv. 4, 11–12, 17–18).[2]

Peter's prophecies prepare the troops for battle; Jude's warnings sound the alarm.

Structure of the Book

Jude's rousing letter has all the elements of a good speech—an introduction (vv. 1–4), a body of thought (vv. 5–23), and a con-clusion (vv. 24–25). The main body can be divided into two parts: *why* we should not follow the false teachers (vv. 5–16) and *how* we can contend against them (vv. 17–23).

Undergirding Jude's appeal is a passionate confidence in the Almighty, who judges the wicked and protects His own. "No-one is more certain than Jude of God's keeping power," declare com-mentators Dick Lucas and Christopher Green.[3] Yet our security in God does not free us to live as we please (which was the error of the apostates). Rather, His power, to keep us safe, compels us to keep ourselves close to Him (see v. 21).

---

2. Bruce Wilkinson and Kenneth Boa, *Talk Thru the Bible* (Nashville, Tenn.: Thomas Nelson Publishers, 1983), p. 502.

3. Dick Lucas and Christopher Green, *The Message of 2 Peter and Jude: The Promise of His Coming*, The Bible Speaks Today Series (Downers Grove, Ill.: InterVarsity Press, 1995), p. 162.

Introduction: Contend for the Faith (vv. 1–4)

Having made his greeting in verses 1–2, Jude introduces his main theme and his reason for writing:

> Beloved, while I was making every effort to write you about our common salvation, I felt the necessity to write to you appealing that you *contend earnestly for the faith* which was once for all delivered to the saints. For certain persons have crept in unnoticed, those who were long beforehand marked out for this condemnation, ungodly persons who turn the grace of our God into licentiousness and deny our only Master and Lord, Jesus Christ. (vv. 3–4, emphasis added)

The Greek word translated "contend earnestly" is *epagonizomai,* and from its root, we get our word *agonize*. The picture is of a wrestler grappling with an opponent, determined not to give up an inch of territory.

The precious ground we must agonize for is "the faith," which is the complete body of Christian truth concerning God, the Bible, Christ, sin, redemption, heaven, and so on. These priceless doctrines were delivered "once for all." They are our absolutes, our solid nucleus of truth that can't be amended, erased, or molded to suit our lifestyle.

Like poison dropped furtively into someone's drink, enemies of the faith had quietly penetrated the church, poisoning the core of Christian truth in at least two ways. First, they turned the grace of God into freedom to indulge the flesh without guilt (compare Rom. 6:15–23). Second, they denied that Jesus was God in the flesh and taught that He represented only one of many stages on the way to God.

Reasons for Not Following the Apostates (vv. 5–16)

Instead of getting mired in a debate over issues, Jude takes his readers to a higher plane, God's perspective, and tells them five reasons they should not follow the false teachers.

Because They Are under God's Judgment (vv. 5–7)

The first reason is that these false teachers are on a path to judgment—the same judgment suffered by the unbelieving Israelites, the fallen angels, and the people of Sodom and Gomorrah

(vv. 5–7). We would surely be foolish to follow anyone heading down that road.

Because They Are Blasphemers (vv. 8–10)

The second reason is that these false teachers blaspheme every authority above their own. They shape their thoughts not by divine truth, but by their own "dreams" and faulty opinions. Jude presents a threefold charge against them: they "defile the flesh, and reject authority, and revile angelic majesties" (v. 8).

In verse 9, he illustrates the magnitude of their blasphemies with a story from the Assumption of Moses, an apocryphal book familiar to his readers.[4] According to the account, the archangel Michael was sent to bury Moses' body. When Lucifer intercepted him to claim the body, Michael showed no disrespect to Lucifer but left the matter with the Judge of all creatures, saying, "The Lord rebuke you." The point is, if Michael weighed his words carefully when addressing the wickedest of angels, how presumptuous it is for the apostates to rail against righteous angels!

But their blasphemies go further. According to verse 10, if they don't understand something (the Incarnation, for example), they criticize it. They only accept the things they can grasp with their fleshly minds. They are "like unreasoning animals," unable to judge or to control their appetites. Ironically, it is "by these things they are destroyed" (v. 10).

Because Their Spirituality Is Empty (vv. 11–13)

The third reason not to follow the false teachers is because of their spiritual emptiness. Like self-sufficient Cain, they offer God the fruit of human works rather than trust in the blood of the Lamb (v. 11; see also Gen. 4:1–7; Heb. 9:22; 11:4). Like greedy Balaam, they sell their prophecies for profit (see Num. 22; Deut. 23:3–4; Neh. 13:2; 2 Pet. 2:15–16). And like rebellious Korah, they defy the authority of God's chosen vessels of truth—Christ and His apostles (see Num. 16:1–33).[5]

---

4. By citing familiar extrabiblical passages, Jude was merely adding punch and relevance to his points, much like Paul did when he quoted the Greek poet Aratus in his address to the intellectuals at Mars Hill (see Acts 17:28). Quoting a work doesn't make it inspired Scripture.

5. No matter how reasonable its words or winsome its ways, apostasy is diametrically opposed to Christ. Instead of the *way* of Christ, there is the way of Cain. Instead of the *truth* of Christ, there is the error of Balaam. Instead of the *life* of Christ, there is the death of Korah.

In verses 12–13, Jude vividly describes the dangers of their religion. Like "hidden reefs," they shipwreck others' faith in the most sacred area, the Lord's Supper. Like "clouds without water," they have nothing real to offer a thirsting soul. Like "autumn trees without fruit, doubly dead, uprooted," they don't nourish the spirit's deepest hunger. Like "wild waves of the sea" pounding a shoreline, they erode others' character and send up a spray of immorality for all to see. And like "wandering" or shooting stars, which shine "briefly, and then vanish without producing light or giving direction,"[6] they lead others astray and then disappear in the darkness of judgment.

Because Their Ways Are Ungodly (vv. 14–16)

For the final reason, Jude makes his point by quoting another apocryphal book, Enoch.

> It was also about these men that Enoch, in the seventh generation from Adam, prophesied, saying, "Behold, the Lord came with many thousands of His holy ones, to execute judgment upon all, and to convict all the ungodly of all their ungodly deeds which they have done in an ungodly way, and of all the harsh things which ungodly sinners have spoken against Him." (vv. 14–15)

With these verses, Jude tears off the apostates' pious masks, revealing hideous scars of lust, arrogance, and greed (v. 16). The exact opposite of the spiritual pedagogues they say they are—they're ungodly.

How to Contend with the Apostates (vv. 17–23)

Having exposed the true nature of the enemy, Jude briefs his soldiers on God's strategy for battle.

Remember the Training Manual (vv. 17–19)

In the training manual of Scripture, the apostles forewarned that "'In the last time there shall be mockers, following after their

6. Edward C. Pentecost, "Jude," in *The Bible Knowledge Commentary*, New Testament edition, ed. John F. Walvoord and Roy B. Zuck (Wheaton, Ill.: Scripture Press Publications, Victor Books, 1983), p. 922.

own ungodly lusts'" (Jude 18; see 1 Tim. 4:1–2 and 2 Pet. 3:3–4). Anticipating the enemy takes away their surprise advantage. And if we can spot them under their camouflage, the battle is half over. Jude tells us to watch for five characteristics of church-destroying apostates: they are *mockers, immoral, divisive, worldly-minded,* and *devoid of the Spirit* (vv. 18–19).

Keep in Shape (vv. 20–21)

Jude knows that the real battle between truth and error is waged not in the church or the classroom but in the soul. Satan points his arrows of false doctrine right at our hearts and appeals to our deepest needs with lies made to look as appealing as the truth. The only way to discern the devil's counterfeits is to experience the real thing. So Jude instructs the troops, "Keep yourselves in the love of God" (v. 21a). He knows that when we are satisfied in God, Satan's lies lose their power. And his arrows fall harmlessly at our feet.

How do we keep ourselves in God's love? First, by building ourselves up in the faith (v. 20a). This requires that we study the Scriptures to know what we believe. Second, by "praying in the Holy Spirit" (v. 20b). And third, by waiting expectantly for the coming of Christ (v. 21b).

Have Mercy on the War-torn (v. 22)

Under the barrage of false teaching, some will waver in their faith. How should the stronger soldiers respond? By jabbing them with criticism? By abandoning them in disgust? Of course not. Jude tells us, "Have mercy on some, who are doubting" (v. 22).

Save the Defectors (v. 23)

Unfortunately, there will be some who defect to the other side. Jude says not to give up hope concerning these but try to save them, in effect, "snatching them out of the fire" (v. 23a). Instead of judging them, we are to "have mercy with fear," knowing that, if it weren't for God's grace, we could be among them on the same road to judgment.[7] And instead of hating them as traitors, we should hate the sin that is destroying them. Jude refers to this as "hating even the garment polluted by the flesh" (v. 23b). Whatever carries the disease of their apostasy, we must not touch.

---

7. Apostatized believers will not lose their salvation but will endure the Lord's discipline, which may include physical death. At the believers' judgment, all their works will be destroyed, and they will suffer great loss (see 1 Cor. 3:10–15).

Benediction: Assurance of Victory (vv. 24–25)

Jude concludes his speech with a stirring benediction that communicates God's unfailing protection:

> Now to Him who is able to keep you from stumbling, and to make you stand in the presence of His glory blameless with great joy, to the only God our Savior, through Jesus Christ our Lord, be glory, majesty, dominion and authority, before all time and now and forever. Amen.

With these words, Jude sends us marching into battle singing the praises of God, confident in His mighty arm of salvation.

Living Insights

As long as the devil has a beachhead in our world, we have to be ready to fight. Unlike a country, though, the church doesn't have civilians who stay home while the military fights the battles. Every citizen of Christ's kingdom is a soldier.

You may not have thought of yourself as a soldier in God's army before, but you are. And as a soldier, your performance on the battlefield depends on your training. Have you received any spiritual training since becoming a Christian? If so, in what areas (Bible knowledge, prayer, doctrine, worship, service, etc.)?

_____

_____

In which areas do you need more training?

_____

_____

Take a minute to plan out a program for yourself. It may be as simple as reading a book, listening to a tape series as you drive to work, or keeping a prayer journal.

My Spiritual Training Plan

_____

_____

_____

_____

_____

_____

_____

_____

_____

_____

Whatever program we devise, Jude reminds us of the ultimate goal for every soldier of Christ: to "keep yourselves in the love of God" (v. 21). Satan, with the powers of hell at his disposal, has yet to devise a weapon that can penetrate the defenses of God's love.

Chapter 14

REVELATION: GOD'S FINAL WORDS

A Survey of Revelation

With the roll of the timpani, the symphony of Scripture prepares for the grandest of all finales: the return of Christ.

Remember how the symphony began in Genesis? The promise of a deliverer was first given as the "seed" of the woman who will crush the serpent's head (Gen. 3:15). The hope was passed on to Abraham, who passed it on to his son Isaac, who passed it on to his son Jacob, who passed it on to his sons. Then it was beautifully illustrated in the Exodus. It was longed for by the judges, amplified in the kings, and predicted by the prophets. Finally, it was fulfilled in the Gospels. But not until the book of Revelation does the theme come to its fullest climax. Christ rides out of heaven to destroy sin and Satan and to restore creation to its original glory for our good and His good pleasure forever.

Hardly a book of fantasies, Revelation cuts to the heart of our deepest yearnings and questions about life. Why are we here? Where is our mixed-up, out-of-control world heading? It reassures us that we're not crazy—something *is* missing in our lives. Things are *not* the way they should be. It's OK to feel dissatisfied with this world, because we were created for a better one. A world without pain. A world of perfect harmony with our Creator and each other. A world that could come at any moment, when Christ appears.

The Writer and His Times

The book opens with these important words about the Author:

> The Revelation of Jesus Christ, which God gave
> Him to show to His bond-servants, the things which
> must soon take place; and He sent and communicated
> it by His angel to His bond-servant John. (Rev. 1:1)

Although the apostle John wrote down the words, Jesus was the real author. Through an angel, Jesus communicated to John God's message in a vision. This vision came to John around A.D. 96, while he was exiled on the island of Patmos for preaching the Gospel.

REVELATION

"I am the Alpha . . ." (1:8) — ". . . and the Omega" (22:13)

	"The things which you have seen . . ."	"The things which are . . ."	"The things which will take place . . ." (Rev. 1:19)
	Personal and biographical	Christ's letters to the seven churches	Christ as Judge (chaps. 4–5) The Tribulation (chaps. 6–18) The Coming of Christ (chap. 19) The Millennium (chap. 20) The Eternal State (chaps. 21–22)
	CHAPTER 1	CHAPTERS 2–3	CHAPTERS 4–22
Scope	History: looking back		Prophecy: looking ahead
Style	Dialogue		Observations and questions
Scene	On earth		Shifts between earth and heaven
Main Theme	Christ's future triumph over the forces of evil and His re-creation of the world for the redeemed		
Key Verses	1:7, 19; 22:12–13		

These were troubled times for the early church. The Roman emperor Domitian considered himself a god and demanded worship from his subjects. Each year, festivals were held throughout the empire in which the citizens were required to offer incense to Caesar and proclaim him as lord.

This practice put Christians in a desperate dilemma. Recognizing Caesar as lord meant denying their true King, Jesus Christ. Yet refusing Caesar was considered an act of disloyalty to Rome, and the consequences were persecution and even death.

"It was to encourage men in such times that the *Revelation* was written," writes commentator William Barclay. "John did not shut his eyes to the terrors; he saw dreadful things and he saw still more dreadful things on the way; but beyond them he saw glory for those who defied Caesar for the love of Christ."[1]

Four Views of Revelation

Of all the books in Scripture, Revelation is the most glorious . . . and perplexing. The terrible, multiheaded beasts; the cosmic upheaval; the spectral battles; the sky-splitting displays of supernatural power. How are we to make sense of it?

Through the centuries, interpreters have taken four approaches to unlocking Revelation's mysteries. *Idealists* view the images nonliterally, as spiritualized symbols that represent timeless truths—for example, the victory of good over evil. *Preterists* (from *praeter*, meaning "past") limit the meaning of the book to its original readers, saying the images represent only first-century subjects, such as Caesar, Rome, and the persecution. They believe that the events have already taken place. *Historicists* see the book as a historical timeline from the first century on. The churches in chapters 2–3, for example, depict seven periods of church history. *Futurists* view the book (primarily chapters 4–22) as a window to the end of time. The images symbolize the people and events that will play key roles in the final drama of world history.

Which approach do we take? By comparing Revelation with the rest of Scripture, particularly the prophecies of Daniel and

---

1. William Barclay, *The Revelation of John*, rev. ed., The Daily Study Bible Series (Philadelphia, Pa.: Westminster Press, 1976), vol. 1, pp. 19–20.

Jesus,[2] we find that the futurists' path is the best approach. However, in all our talk about the future, let's not forget the meaning of the text to its original readers or its timeless truths for us today.

Literary Style

Revelation's apocalyptic style seems strange to us, but in John's day, it was fairly common. It was not meant to mystify its intended audience but rather reveal encouraging truth to them. The Greek word for *revelation*, in fact, is *apokalupsis*, which means "an uncovering, laying bare."[3] For those enduring persecution, apocalyptic literature uncovered a future in which creation would experience rebirth—a time when the ugliness of "this present age" would be transformed into the glory of "the age to come." And this change would not come through human hands but through the direct intervention of God.

What an awesome thought! It almost defies description. That's why, as Barclay explains, "All apocalyptic literature is necessarily cryptic. It is continually attempting to describe the indescribable, to say the unsayable, to paint the unpaintable."[4]

Since to us, so many centuries later, the language and symbols are especially cryptic, it will be helpful to follow a few guidelines. First, *don't overanalyze the details*. It's easy to lose the central message by wandering into speculations about what the mark of the Beast will be or whose name totals 666. John interprets many of the symbols for us, and we should stay focused on what he says.

Second, *be careful not to read too much of our world into the text*. John was not a time traveler, beamed into the future by God. The locusts and hail probably aren't John's attempts to describe fighter jets and nuclear fallout in first-century terms. Try to avoid the temptation of correlating every image to a modern equivalent. Instead, look for connections in other parts of Scripture, like the ten

---

2. Many of the symbols in Daniel's visions reappear in John's, such as the lion, bear, leopard, and beast (compare Dan. 7 and Rev. 13). The catastrophic time in Revelation 6–18 closely aligns with Daniel's seventieth week (Dan. 9:27) and Jesus' "great tribulation" (Matt. 24:15–27). Also, the Second Coming in Revelation 1:17 and 19:11–21 parallels Daniel 7:11–14, 21–27 and Matthew 24:29–31.

3. G. Abbott-Smith, *A Manual Greek Lexicon of the New Testament*, 3d ed. (Edinburgh, Scotland: T. and T. Clark, 1937), p. 50.

4. Barclay, *The Revelation of John*, p. 4.

plagues of Egypt, for example, which would have meant more to the original readers.

Third, *emphasize the message behind the image.* For example, John describes Christ as having "a sharp two-edged sword" coming out of His mouth (Rev. 1:16; 19:15). We are not to take this literally. The important thing for us is the meaning that the image communicates—that is, Christ is coming with judgment.

Central Figure of the Book

As the final word of Scripture, Revelation unveils the central figure of Scripture in all His glory: Jesus Christ. He is the Savior to whom all the symbols point, as we will see in our unfolding study.

To miss seeing Christ in Revelation is like squinting into the noontime sky and not seeing the sun. His presence radiates everywhere. And you might be surprised to find that Revelation, though a little intimidating at first, is the most worshipful book in the Bible. For it reveals the glorious splendor of our gracious Lord.

The Structure of the Book

We can outline Revelation in at least two ways. One way is to organize the book as a series of sevens. After an introductory section (chap. 1), the book divides like this:

- The seven churches, 2:1–3:22

- The seven seals, 4:1–8:1

- The seven trumpets, 8:2–11:19

- The seven signs in heaven, 12:1–15:8

- The seven bowls of wrath, 16:1–21

- The seven final visions, 17:1–22:21[5]

Another way is to divide the book in three broad parts, according to the pattern in 1:19:

"Therefore write the things which you have seen,

5. John Stott, *Men with a Message: An Introduction to the New Testament and Its Writers*, revised by Stephen Motyer (Grand Rapids, Mich.: William B. Eerdmans Publishing Co., 1994), p. 147.

and the things which are, and the things which will
take place after these things."

The three phrases in this verse mark the progression of the book. "The things which you have seen" reviews the past, how John received the revelation (chap. 1). "The things which are" records the present, Christ's messages to the seven churches (chaps. 2–3). And "the things which will take place after these things" reveals the future in the four culminating events of world history: the Tribulation, Christ's return, the Millennium, and eternity (chaps. 4–22).[6]

We'll base our survey on this second approach, highlighting the recurring sevens as we go.

"The Things Which You Have Seen" (Chap. 1)

The first sight we see is Jesus, who is both the Revealer and the One revealed (1:1a). The message from Christ is urgent because "the time is near" (v. 3b). The end could come at any moment.

This letter is addressed to the seven churches in Asia (and, generally, to all believers). It arrives by special angelic delivery from God and "the seven Spirits"—or "the sevenfold Spirit," which is the Holy Spirit—and Jesus Christ. Jesus has authority over all realms, both the kingdoms of the earth and the spiritual kingdom of believers, whom He has purified with His blood for priestly service to God (vv. 4–6). Verses 7–8 announce the main theme of the book:

> Behold, He is coming with the clouds, and every eye will see Him, even those who pierced Him; and all the tribes of the earth will mourn over Him. So it is to be. Amen.
>
> "I am the Alpha and the Omega," says the Lord God, "who is and who was and who is to come, the Almighty."

John's vision of seven golden lampstands represents the seven churches. In the middle of them stands the Light of the church, Jesus Christ, arrayed in splendor and strength. At the sight of Him,

---

6. Based on Bruce Wilkinson and Kenneth Boa's outline in *Talk Thru the Bible* (Nashville, Tenn.: Thomas Nelson Publishers, 1983), pp. 518–20.

John collapses as if dead. Touching him reassuringly, Jesus gives him seven messages, one for each of the seven churches (vv. 9–20).

"The Things Which Are" (Chaps. 2–3)

In his reflective book on Revelation, Eugene Peterson identifies a pattern in Jesus' messages: "There is, first, a positive affirmation; second, a corrective discipline; and third, a motivating promise."[7] Two of the churches, Sardis and Laodicea, are given no affirmation; and two others, Smyrna and Philadelphia, receive no discipline. Generally, Jesus confronts indifference, toleration of sin, apathy, and self-sufficiency. His words are hard to hear; but after them, like a refreshing spring rain, come words of hope. To those who "overcome," who endure to the end, Jesus promises the rewards of eternal life—which are gloriously displayed in chapters 21–22.

Endure to the end—that's the essence of Jesus' message to the churches in Asia. To amplify that theme, in the next prophetic section of the book He reveals the future, not to satisfy their curiosity, but to further encourage their faithfulness.

"The Things Which Will Take Place" (Chaps. 4–22)

The Worthy Lamb (Chaps. 4–5)

The vision continues as Christ ushers John into the throne room of God, the birthplace of creation and the locus of all that is and will be. In the very center sits God, reigning in absolute authority. The glistening colors and resonating sounds of worship saturate John's senses, and in one wonderful moment he experiences the purpose for which humankind was created—union with God. Yet that purpose cannot be realized for the world until someone opens the book of God's plan of the ages. Only one Person is worthy, Jesus Christ, who is pictured as a slain lamb. Why a lamb? Because only through His sacrificial atonement is our future with God possible.

The Tribulation (6:1–19:5)

Purification must precede worship, and that is the main objective of the Tribulation period—to cleanse the creation for its Creator and to draw to Him as many as will come.

---

7. Eugene H. Peterson, *Reversed Thunder: The Revelation of John and the Praying Imagination* (San Francisco, Calif.: HarperCollins Publishers, HarperSanFrancisco, 1988), p. 50.

Seals, trumpets, and bowls (chaps. 6; 8–9; 11:15–19; 16). By opening the first seal of the book, Christ initiates three sets of seven judgments: the seal judgments (chap. 6; 8:1), the trumpet judgments (chaps. 8–9; 11:15–19), and the bowl judgments (chap. 16). These judgments can be viewed as sequential events: the seventh seal unleashes the seven trumpets, and the seventh trumpet unleashes the seven bowls. Or we can see them as cycles, with each set of judgments spanning the whole Tribulation period but gradually progressing forward to the grand climax of Christ's return.

In either case, as the judgments progress, they grow in intensity and frequency. By the end, they fall like hammer blows. Pestilence, famine, earthquakes, plagues—the world reels under their combined impact. Sadly, even these terrible displays of God's power do not break the people's hardened hearts, and like Pharaoh, they refuse to

> repent of the works of their hands, so as not to worship demons, and the idols of gold and of silver and of brass and of stone and of wood, which can neither see nor hear nor walk; and they did not repent of their murders nor of their sorceries nor of their immorality nor of their thefts. (9:20–21)

Sealing the saints, the little book, and the two witnesses (chaps. 7; 10:1–11:14). Does John see any godliness during the Tribulation? Yes, a select number of Jews come to faith ("the 144,000"), whom God seals for salvation (7:1–8). Another godly group is the great multitude of martyrs who die for the sake of Christ. John sees them standing in heaven, praising God and receiving their reward (7:9–17).

Two additional heavenly influences are the Word of God (the "little book") that is delivered by a mighty angel (chap. 10) and two unidentified "witnesses" (11:3), patterned after Elijah and Moses, who preach Christ. The witnesses are killed for their testimony, but God raises them to life and takes them to heaven as a demonstration of His saving power. Through all means possible, He appeals to the world to be saved, but the world turns away. And when the seventh trumpet blows, the hour of God's wrath has come (chap. 11).

The seven signs (chaps. 12–15). Chapters 12–15 interrupt the sequence of events to describe seven signs or personages. John introduces each with the word *sign* or with the phrase "then I saw" or its equivalent.

The first three signs appear in chapters 12–13: the dragon (Satan) who opposes the woman, the beast out of the sea (the Antichrist), and the beast out of the earth (the False Prophet). These three represent a kind of unholy trinity, a parody of the Father, Son, and Holy Spirit.[8] Instead of the Creator, *Satan* is the Destroyer, who tries to murder the "child" (the Messiah) and the "woman" (Israel). The *Antichrist* mimics the Son of God as he feigns death from a "fatal wound" and then appears to be resurrected. And the *False Prophet* plays the role of the Holy Spirit, as he performs miracles and seals the followers of the beast with a mark on their right hand and forehead.

Chapter 14 unveils three more signs, which focus on God's work during the Tribulation. Christ leads the 144,000 purified Jews, who bear *the* mark of the *Lamb* on their foreheads (vv. 1–5). Three angels proclaim the Gospel and again warn of God's impending wrath (vv. 6–13). Finally, after everyone has heard the Gospel and had their chance to be saved, the "son of man" and an angel swing their sickles and harvest the earth in judgment (vv. 14–20).

The seventh sign appears in chapter 15. Seven angels emerge from the tabernacle where God's Law is stored. They pour out the seven bowl judgments that contain the full measure of God's wrath (see chap. 16).

The fall of Babylon (17:1–19:5). Another feature of the Tribulation period is a mighty religious/political system referred to as "the great harlot" and "Babylon the great" (17:1, 5). This is perhaps a revived Roman empire that, like its ancient ancestor, rules over many nations and violently persecutes Christians. Her influence and wealth flourish during the first half of the seven-year Tribulation; but when the Antichrist rises to power, he destroys her and takes command of the earth for the final three and a half years (vv. 15–18; see also Dan. 7:19–25).

At the fall of Babylon (Rev. 18), heaven erupts in praise of God (19:1–5). This is the signal that "the marriage supper of the Lamb" (v. 9) is near. Christ has received His "bride," the church, at the Rapture (see Eph. 5:22–32; 1 Thess. 4:13–18). Now the wedding banquet is about to commence . . . but first, the Bridegroom must destroy the Destroyer.

8. See Stott, *Men with a Message*, p. 151.

131

The Coming of Christ and the Millennial Kingdom (19:6–20:15)

At His first coming, Jesus slipped into the world as a tiny baby born in Bethlehem. Now He rides out of heaven as a mighty warrior, the "King of Kings and Lord of Lords" (Rev. 19:16), saddled on a white horse with eyes ablaze, wielding a sword of judgment. With a mighty clash, He unleashes the fury of God's wrath upon the forces of the earth that have gathered against Him at Armageddon ("Har-Magedon," 16:16). After wiping out His enemies, He casts the Antichrist and the False Prophet into the lake of fire (19:7–21).

Satan's doom, however, comes later. Christ binds him for a thousand years while He fulfills the kingdom promises to Israel and reigns on the earth over the surviving Tribulation saints (20:1–3). The dead Tribulation saints are resurrected in what John calls "the first resurrection" (vv. 4–6).

As children are born during the Millennium, though, not everyone submits to Christ. And at the end of the Millennial Age, Satan is released to lead one last charge against the city of God. At the battle of "Gog and Magog," fire bursts out of heaven to consume Satan's army (vv. 8–9), and, finally, Satan is "thrown into the lake of fire and brimstone, where the beast and the false prophet are also; and they will be tormented day and night forever and ever" (v. 10).

In the next scene, God is sitting upon "a great white throne." Standing before this throne are all the dead unbelievers throughout history who have been resurrected to face their final judgment (vv. 11–15).

The Eternal State (Chaps. 21–22)

With sin and Satan destroyed, God recreates the heavens and the earth, and the story of Scripture comes full circle. Paradise lost is now paradise restored. Rather than a garden, though, God fashions a "holy city, the new Jerusalem" (21:2), in which the redeemed dwell with their God in perfect unity.

> "They will be his people, and God himself will be with them and be their God. He will wipe every tear from their eyes. There will be no more death or mourning or crying or pain, for the old order of things has passed away." (vv. 3b–4 NIV)

132

This is *eternal life*, the reward that God freely offers those who overcome the world through faith in Christ (v. 7).

Why are we here? Where is our mixed-up, out-of-control world heading? Revelation answers these questions, and so much more. When the hardness of life leaves us bruised and battered, Revelation offers a hope to hold on to. When the best of the world's pleasures leave us thirsting for true satisfaction and inner peace, this book beckons us to come "take the water of life without cost" (22:17).

Are you weary? Are you in pain? "I am coming quickly," Jesus promises three times in the final chapter (vv. 7, 12, 20). With breathless anticipation, we answer: "Amen. Come, Lord Jesus" (v. 20b).

 Living Insights

In *Talk Thru the Bible*, Bruce Wilkinson and Kenneth Boa tie together the first and last three chapters of Scripture with some insightful contrasts.[9] Reflect on their observations.

Genesis 1–3	Revelation 20–22
"In the beginning God created the heavens and the earth" (1:1)	"I saw a new heaven and a new earth" (21:1)
"The darkness He called Night" (1:5)	"There shall be no night there" (21:25)
"God made two great lights" (sun and moon; 1:16)	"The city had no need of the sun or of the moon" (21:23)
"In the day that you eat of it you shall surely die" (2:17)	"There shall be no more death" (21:4)
Satan appears as deceiver of mankind (3:1)	Satan disappears forever (20:10)
Shown a garden into which defilement entered (3:6–7)	Shown a city into which defilement will never enter (21:27)
Walk of God with man interrupted (3:8–10)	Walk of God with man resumed (21:3)
Initial triumph of the serpent (3:13)	Ultimate triumph of the Lamb (20:10; 22:3)

9. Wilkinson and Boa, *Talk Thru the Bible*, p. 515.

Genesis 1–3	Revelation 20–22
"I will greatly multiply your sorrow" (3:16)	"There shall be no more death or sorrow, nor crying; and there shall be no more pain" (21:4)
"Cursed is the ground for your sake" (3:17)	"There shall be no more curse" (22:3)
Man's dominion broken in the fall of the first man, Adam (3:19)	Man's dominion restored in the rule of the new man, Christ (22:5)
First paradise closed (3:23)	New paradise opened (21:25)
Access to the tree of life disinherited in Adam (3:24)	Access to the tree of life reinstated in Christ (22:14)
They were driven from God's presence (3:24)	"They shall see His face" (22:4)

The Bible is the story of how God bridged the gap between the cursed life and the glorious life through our redemption in Christ. We believe that the story is true, but the problem is we've only known the hard-edged reality of the cursed world. The glorious world seems so distant.

That's why Christ gave us the book of Revelation, to bring the hope near, to spark our imaginations and make the vision real. As you conclude this survey of Scripture, take a few moments to read the last three chapters of the Bible. How do the images touch the deepest yearnings of your heart? Feel free to draw your study to a close with words of worship to our magnificent Lord.

_____

_____

_____

_____

_____

_____

_____

BOOKS FOR
PROBING FURTHER

What a finale! What a concert! One we hope you'll remember for a long time. The music of *God's Masterwork* doesn't have to end here, though. We hope that these five volumes will serve only as a prelude to your own deeper study of God's Word.

For further reflection on 2 Thessalonians through Revelation, we recommend the following resources. May they help God's melody of grace linger on throughout your life.

Biographical Studies

Gill, David W. *Peter the Rock: Extraordinary Insights from an Ordinary Man*. Downers Grove, Ill.: InterVarsity Press, 1986.

Pollock, John. *The Apostle: A Life of Paul*. Wheaton, Ill.: Scripture Press Publications, Victor Books, 1985.

Stott, John. *Men with a Message: An Introduction to the New Testament and Its Writers*. Revised by Stephen Motyer. Grand Rapids, Mich.: William B. Eerdmans Publishing Co., 1994.

Commentaries and Biblical Reference

Clowney, Edmund P. *The Message of 1 Peter: The Way of the Cross*. The Bible Speaks Today Series. Downers Grove, Ill.: InterVarsity Press, 1988.

Gaebelein, Frank E., gen. ed. *The Expositor's Bible Commentary*. Vols. 11, 12. Grand Rapids, Mich.: Zondervan Publishing House, Regency Reference Library, 1978, 1981.

Jackman, David. *The Message of John's Letters: Living in the Love of God*. The Bible Speaks Today Series. Downers Grove, Ill.: InterVarsity Press, 1988.

Lucas, Dick, and Christopher Green. *The Message of 2 Peter and Jude: The Promise of His Coming*. The Bible Speaks Today Series. Downers Grove, Ill.: InterVarsity Press, 1995.

Peterson, Eugene H. *Reversed Thunder: The Revelation of John and the Praying Imagination.* San Francisco, Calif.: HarperSanFrancisco, 1988. Though not a verse-by-verse commentary, Peterson's reflective exploration of Revelation's themes and thrust is highly recommended for anyone wanting to understand what Revelation is all about.

Towner, Philip H. *1–2 Timothy and Titus.* The IVP New Testament Commentary Series. Downers Grove, Ill.: InterVarsity Press, 1994.

Walvoord, John F., and Roy B. Zuck, eds. *The Bible Knowledge Commentary.* New Testament ed. Wheaton, Ill.: Scripture Press Publications, Victor Books, 1983.

Webster, Douglas D. *Finding Spiritual Direction: The Challenge and Joys of Christian Growth.* Downers Grove, Ill.: InterVarsity Press, 1991. This book is also not a verse-by-verse commentary but focuses on the spiritual direction provided by James. It will be an invaluable help to your study of this letter and to your maturity in Christ.

Wilcock, Michael. *The Message of Revelation: I Saw Heaven Opened.* The Bible Speaks Today Series. Downers Grove, Ill.: InterVarsity Press, 1975.

Wilkinson, Bruce, and Kenneth Boa. *Talk Thru the Bible.* Nashville, Tenn.: Thomas Nelson Publishers, 1983. An outstanding survey that captures the themes and direction of every book of the Bible.

Thematic Studies

Character and Leadership

Bridges, Jerry. *The Pursuit of Holiness.* Colorado Springs, Colo.: NavPress, 1978.

Getz, Gene A. *The Measure of a Man.* Glendale, Calif.: Gospel Light Publications, Regal Books, 1974.

Hughes, R. Kent. *Disciplines of a Godly Man.* Wheaton, Ill.: Good News Publishers, Crossway Books, 1991.

Sanders, J. Oswald. *Spiritual Leadership.* Rev. ed. Chicago, Ill.: Moody Press, 1980.

Christ, Grace, and Law

Bridges, Jerry. *Transforming Grace: Living Confidently in God's Unfailing Love.* Colorado Springs, Colo.: NavPress, 1991.

Horton, Michael, ed. *Christ the Lord: The Reformation and Lordship Salvation.* Grand Rapids, Mich.: Baker Book House, 1992.

Luther, Martin. *The Bondage of the Will.* Trans. J. I. Packer and O. R. Johnston. Grand Rapids, Mich.: Baker Book House, Fleming H. Revell, 1957.

Sproul, R. C. *The Glory of Christ.* Wheaton, Ill.: Tyndale House Publishers, 1990.

End Times

Benware, Paul N. *Understanding End Times Prophecy: A Comprehensive Approach.* Chicago, Ill.: Moody Press, 1995.

Conyers, A. J. *The End: What Jesus Really Said about the Last Things.* Downers Grove, Ill.: InterVarsity Press, 1995.

Hoekema, Anthony A. *The Bible and the Future.* Grand Rapids, Mich.: William B. Eerdmans Publishing Co., 1979.

False Teachers

Abanes, Richard. *Defending the Faith: A Beginner's Guide to Cults and New Religions.* Grand Rapids, Mich.: Baker Book House, Baker Books, 1997.

Hanegraaff, Hank. *Christianity in Crisis.* Eugene, Oreg.: Harvest House Publishers, 1993.

Suffering

Kreeft, Peter. *Making Sense Out of Suffering.* Ann Arbor, Mich.: Servant Books, 1986.

Sproul, R. C. *Surprised by Suffering.* Wheaton, Ill.: Tyndale House Publishers, 1988.

Insight for Living also has study guides available on 1 and 2 Thessalonians, 1 Timothy, Philemon, Hebrews, James, 1 and 2 Peter, 2 and 3 John, Jude, and Revelation 1–3. For more information, see the ordering instructions that follow and contact the office that serves you.

Some of the books listed may be out of print and available only through a library. For those currently available, please contact your local Christian bookstore. Books by Charles R. Swindoll may be obtained through Insight for Living, as well as some books by other authors. Just call the IFL office that serves you

ORDERING INFORMATION

GOD'S MASTERWORK
Volume Five

If you would like to order additional study guides, purchase the cassette series that accompanies this guide, or request our product catalogs, please contact the office that serves you.

United States and International locations:

Insight for Living
Post Office Box 69000
Anaheim, CA 92817-0900

1-800-772-8888, 24 hours a day, 7 days a week
(714) 575-5000, 8:00 A.M. to 4:30 P.M., Pacific time, Monday to Friday

Canada:

Insight for Living Ministries
Post Office Box 2510
Vancouver, BC, Canada V6B 3W7

1-800-663-7639, 24 hours a day, 7 days a week

Australia:

Insight for Living, Inc.
General Post Office Box 2823 EE
Melbourne, VIC 3001, Australia

(03) 9877-4277, 8:30 A.M. to 5:00 P.M., Monday to Friday

World Wide Web:
www.insight.org

Study Guide Subscription Program

Study guide subscriptions are available. Please call or write the office nearest you to find out how you can receive our study guides on a regular basis.